The Fine Art of Recuperation

Also by the author:

Wellness Workbook (with John W. Travis, M.D.)

The Fine Art
of Recuperation

A Guide to Surviving and Thriving after
Illness, Accident, or Surgery

REGINA SARA RYAN

Foreword by John W. Travis, M.D.

JEREMY P. TARCHER, INC.
Los Angeles

Excerpt from *Tao Te Ching* by Lao Tsu, edited by Gia-Fu Feng, translated by Jane English. Copyright © 1972. Reprinted by permission of Alfred A. Knopf, Inc.

Calligraphy for "Crisis is Danger and Opportunity" by Chungliang Al Huang, President, Living Tao Foundation, P.O. Box 846, Urbana, IL 61801. All rights reserved.

"How carefully was that word chosen" from *Still Life with Woodpecker* by Tom Robbins, copyright © 1980 by Tibetan Peach Pie, Inc. Reprinted by permission of Bantam Books, a division of Bantam, Doubleday, Dell Publishing Group, Inc.

Library of Congress Cataloging in Publication Data

Ryan, Regina Sara.
    The fine art of recuperation: a guide to surviving and thriving
  after illness, accident or surgery / Regina Sara Ryan.
p.   cm.
    Bibliography.
    1. Sick—Psychology. 2. Healing. 3. Convalescence. I. Title.
R726.5.R9 1989
616'.001'9—dc19
    ISBN 0-87477-511-6   89-31181
                                                          CIP

Copyright © 1989 by Regina Sara Ryan
Foreword copyright © 1989 by John W. Travis

Jeremy P. Tarcher, Inc.
9110 Sunset Blvd.
Los Angeles, CA 90069

Distributed by St. Martin's Press, New York

Design by Tanya Maiboroda

Manufactured in the United States of America
10 9 8 7 6 5 4 3 2 1
First Edition

To Jere

Contents

Suffering is a divine favor in disguise.

CHINESE PROVERB

Not in his goals but in his transitions man is great.

RALPH WALDO EMERSON

Repair can bring exceptional progress.

I CHING, BOOK OF CHANGES

At the point when everything is out of control one can still choose what attitude to have toward the experience—to become bitter, or to keep the human spirit alive . . .

JEAN SHINODA BOLEN, M.D.

Acknowledgments

This book went through several false labors before its birth. And with each of them I had the support and wisdom of many friends, students, and family members. I wish to express heartfelt thanks to them:

My husband and best friend, Jere Pramuk, for paying the bills and everything else.

Jim and Ruth Sharon, Lloyd Barde, Laurie Campion and Kris Rebillot, and especially Barry Tellman, who inspired the early steps in the process.

Darso and all who nursed me back to health in Denver, and to Roselyn Smith and others who took care of me in India.

Anita Jordan, who supported me in countless ways when I lost it all; Dr. Jim Blessman, who helped me turn a corner; Dr. John Travis, for ongoing friendship and door opening.

Mia Ryan, whose input got me started again on the right track, and Louise Hart, who helped me to remember that I still had a contribution to make.

Kate Fotopoulos, the midwife extraordinaire, who said, "As long as there is a greater intelligence out there, why not use it?" Our debt will never be settled.

Joelle Carelli-Hedden, for her gracious research assistance.

My parents, Bernard and Helene Ryan.

Jeremy Tarcher, my publisher, for his vision; Rick Benzel, my editor, for his active partnership with me.

All the friends and recuperating people whose stories are related here, and for the many others who spoke to me about what they learned from their crises.

My beloved spiritual Master, Mr. Lee Lozowick, for his benediction, his humor, and his music.

Foreword

I am delighted that this book has finally been born. From the time Regina first shared the idea with me, I saw the need for it. Now that it has been published, I am even more enthusiastic about it. Like the I-V bottle hanging over the bed, this book is filled with a vitality that infuses the reader with renewed energy and inspiration.

Medicine over the past five decades has fostered the myth that there is a pill for every ill. We look to external authorities for the answers to everything, including our health. We are subtly encouraged to deny the wisdom of our own body and the incredible power of our own internal healing mechanisms. More and more people are seeing the limitations of thinking that modern medicine *alone* can provide all our answers. We are being forced to look inward and to reclaim our own abilities to heal and be whole. This book takes us a long way toward reclaiming those abilities.

My father is a doctor in a small town in the Midwest. The medical treatment he offers his patients is full of care and concern for their personal well-being. He knows all his patients and their family histories. I grew up wanting to help people like my father did. But when I went to medical school in Boston I was shocked to learn that here medicine was very different from what I had seen my father practice. Here the emphasis was on diagnosis and treatment of *diseases,* not people. As medical students we discussed not Mrs. O'Connell, but "the cancer" in room 410; not Harvey Bernstein, but "the broken leg" in room 212.

Even when I decided to pursue a residency in preventive medicine at Johns Hopkins in the early seventies, I was still acutely aware that something vital was lacking in our approach to illness and health. That's when I discovered a little-known book on wellness by a little-known doctor named Halbert Dunn. Dunn envisioned wellness as the synthesis of the psychological, emotional, and spiritual states of health with the physical states.

Inspired by Dunn, I decided to give up my plans of practicing medicine and work full-time in further developing this unknown field of wellness. Several years later I opened the first Wellness Center (Mill Valley, 1975). There are now several thousand such centers scattered across the country, and the numbers are growing around the world as well.

I can speak from years of experience with people caught in a problem-orientation toward life and health. I know that illness is a multifaceted phenomenon, and that working with the body, the thinking, the sense of humor, the sense of meaning, the support by others, is necessary to healing into wholeness. Through my work I met Regina, and in 1980 we coauthored the *Wellness Workbook.* While my work in wellness has filled much of what I believed to be lacking in today's health care, many gaps still remain. *The Fine Art of Recuperation,* in approaching illness from a wellness perspective and providing tools and inspiration for those who are sick, has filled one very major gap.

While I've delved professionally into the origins of physical (and mental) maladies for over twenty years, some of my most important lessons have come with my own experiences of being laid up. A back problem continues to surface when I am not taking good care of myself. I have come to recognize it as an internal cue inviting me to start paying more attention. Still, it's humiliating for a wellness pioneer to admit to these "failings" and even more humiliating to struggle with the guilt that surfaces whenever I am ill. *The Fine Art of Recuperation* speaks to me convincingly about this issue. Regina encourages an approach of compassion and self-forgiveness, recognizing the common tendency to equate weakness of any sort with "badness." Her emphasis on illness as a type of loss which brings on the grief process is an important consideration. Few of us recognize how powerful are the interconnections of mind, body, and spirit. It is natural to feel scared, insecure, or even worthless when your body is wounded in some way. Accepting ourselves as hurting human beings who are still basically OK is an essential first step to full healing.

In a world of fast lanes and bottom lines, illness is the great teacher who demands that we reorder our priorities. This book is a wonderful guide to how we may use our experiences with illness, surgery, or "accidents" to become more loving toward ourselves and those around us.

Several months ago, I received a call that one of my dearest friends, Joy, was in a serious car crash and would be undergoing surgery. The news shook me out of my own petty concerns. Illness is a wake-up call to everybody—to friends and family as well as to the patient herself. I wanted to help her, to be there for her in some way. When a call to her husband reassured me she would recover, I did the next best thing I could think of—I sent her a tape of jokes, knowing that she appreciated the healing value of laughter, and I lit a candle to remind me to send prayers and healing thoughts her way. I would have sent her this book were it available.

This book definitely demands attention for people who are laid up and for those around them. It is inexpensive, easy to take (but not sugar-coated), and long lasting, with no harmful side effects. I hope it will be available in every doctor's waiting room. Were doctors to give copies free to their patients, I'm sure it would make their work a more pleasant and effective experience by encouraging readers to join in a practical and gentle partnership for healing.

—John W. Travis, M.D.
Sebastopol, California
July 1989

Introduction

Convalescence, like mourning, is a
lost art.

MIRIAM SIEGLER AND
HUMPHREY OSMOND,
Patienthood

This book is for you or anyone who is temporarily

- laid up,
- laid off, or
- laid back

due to an accident or illness, heart attack, surgery or hospitalization, unemployment, laziness, boredom, frustration, depression, overwork, overweight, or undernourishment.

No matter what your physical limitations may be, if you are reading or hearing this now, you are alive. And to be alive means to be in a state of constant change. This book is for those who are interested in coping and growing and changing and thriving, *in spite of illness.* It is about developing your fullest potential here and now with your limitations. It is ultimately about using the challenge of this crisis in your life as an opportunity.

Bed is a delicious place to be, except when you are ill and want to be anywhere else. Then it becomes a prison. I know. I have been confined to bed many times in the course of my adult life due to accidents, sickness, surgery, and even depression. I am now something of an expert, but it took me a long time to learn.

In the spring of 1981, while traveling in India, I contracted hepatitis. The doctor who diagnosed me prescribed the "3-R treatment." "You must read and rest and relax for three months," he said. (Sound familiar?)

I looked at him in amazement and very calmly said, "No, thank you." First of all, I was convinced that I was a "fast mender." If it took other people three months to recover from hepatitis, I knew I'd be done in a month and a half.

For the next ten days I fought my illness. I played at being brave and strong and told myself that I would prove the doctor wrong. But it didn't work. My discouragement and panic only grew when, day after day, I actually felt weaker. My recovery didn't take three months; it took five—almost all of it in bed.

A few years ago, I had another accident that sent me to bed again for an extended period. It happened during an especially stressful time. Work was difficult, finances were tight, and some important relationships were strained and shaky. "Give me a break" had become one of my daily prayers. Then I fell on the ski slope five days before Christmas, and those words came back to haunt me. I got my break—three places in my left leg. Several weeks in bed were followed by nearly three months of severely restricted mobility.

My doctor sent me home to enjoy "a nice long rest," just as his colleague in India had prescribed years before. But the novelty of R and R wore off in about forty-eight hours. Lying in bed, in pain, with a cast from toe to thigh, needing help even to get to the bathroom, I felt the frustration, humiliation, and discomfort that you too may be experiencing at this time.

And to make matters worse, within a few days I was utterly bored. Television helped for a couple of hours at a time, but after that it wore me down. I was wasting time, and that realization made me more anxious than almost anything else. Friends provided some diversions—bringing over the daily paper or a new magazine, and even sitting and talking for a while—but they offered only temporary relief. As soon as they were gone, I'd slump back into discouragement.

A few years prior to this incident I had written a book on health and well-being, so I was supposed to know how to be a model patient. But now as the days dragged on, I had to admit that whatever I was doing—or not doing—wasn't working. My unhappiness only increased, my frustration was intense, and I saw no progress in my condition. Expert or no expert, I was stuck. Perhaps you too feel this way now.

Many times during those first painful weeks I remembered my mother's words—"Your problems can be your opportunities"—and wondered how to apply them to my own immediate situation. (Mothers are famous for prescriptions like these—like "If you can't always change what is, you can learn to like it" or "When life hands you a lemon, make lemonade.") Hadn't I made similar recommendations to others in my books—attesting to the positive value that disease could have in one's life? I had taught college students for years, especially in courses about grief and loss, how to take a crisis and turn it into a life-enhancing gift. So why wasn't I taking my own words to heart?

The answer is quite simple, in retrospect: It just wasn't time to do that yet. Even though I could intellectually appreciate that Mother was right, I needed to cope with the shock I had suffered first. And that took time.

Being a writer, I used my journal frequently in those early days, listing my complaints, my fears, even writing out my prayers. But I never got the impact of Mother's message so clearly as the morning I picked up my pen and started to make a list entitled "How to Keep from Going Crazy When You Have to Stay in Bed." Seeing that heading staring back at me at the top of a blank page, I felt the first surge of excitement I'd had in weeks. I began to write—ideas, suggestions, projects—one after another, filling page after page. I knew I was onto something!

From my previous work I knew that there were plenty of books on how to "cure" everything from colds to cancer, and more about how to prevent illness through lifestyle changes. But there wasn't much that addressed the specific challenge of having to spend a significant amount of time recuperating in bed or having to alter a high-speed life.

After heart attack or surgery some patients receive a little booklet that discusses how to eat better and what types of exercise to engage in. In looking at a number of these I found that only one paragraph or so might be devoted to the subject of depression:

> All these feelings of depression and anger and worries about your future are very common, but they usually pass within six months as

you gradually begin to accept your illness and find other satisfying activities and work. If they persist, be sure to speak about them to your doctor.

Six months!? I knew from being sick in India that one month can seem like a lifetime. I also knew that the suggestion "Speak to your doctor" often falls short. Many doctors don't have the time or training to handle emotional upsets. Rarely did any of these pamphlets make reference to the humiliation one goes through in having to ask for help, or in relearning how to walk, to talk, to live again.

The more I read, the more I saw what was missing. We were long overdue for a look at the stress of confinement, as well as at the potential for deeper appreciation of life that recovery time could afford. It was time to develop for myself and share with others the fine art of *recuperation.*

So I began to write—for my own encouragement and for yours. I interviewed friends and visitors and asked them how they spent their critical times in bed. I talked with men and women who had recently undergone open-heart surgery or other major operations. I spoke with doctors, nurses, and rehabilitation specialists. I reflected and recalled my own experiences. When I was back on my feet again I questioned my students, people I met on airplanes, folks I met at parties. The discoveries I made about recuperation and the stories and suggestions of many friends and well-wishers make up this book.

Nearly all of the names used are real, as most friends and students were only too happy to share their stories with others. In a few cases names were changed as these were composites of several different people, or several events in one person's life, condensed into one.

The Fine Art of Recuperation reflects my philosophy that an illness or an accident is a type of loss and therefore catalyzes a grieving process within us. And like grief, recuperation has identifiable stages, predictable pitfalls, and some basic principles the knowledge of which can make the trip a bit easier for you.

As I present it here, the fine art of recuperation provides a gentle way of living through the period following accident, illness, or loss so that the body's natural inclinations toward healing and balance are optimally supported. It is a *holistic* process, since it addresses the whole person—physically, emotionally, intellectually, and spiritually. The fine art of recuperation acknowledges the paradox that even in the midst of breakdown we need not become victims of life. Rather it asserts that we can assume a greater degree of responsibility in our own recovery and tip the scales on the side of speedier and more complete healing. Finally, this fine art is built on the principle that our crisis may offer an opportunity for a richer and more satisfying life.

In essence, recuperation is a practical process. That is why I've titled the divisions of this book "steps" rather than chapters. My job has been to arrange these steps in a somewhat logical progression to guide you from your first shock to your first day back on the job or at home.

Admittedly, the steps to recuperation do not always fall into a straight line. Like a mountain climber, the traveler in this process may encounter constant ups and downs or trails that frequently cross over one another. The sequence these steps appear in by no means implies that any particular issue must be handled completely before the next step can be approached. The holistic view that this book takes is based on the fact that everything is connected. The way you eat or exercise, for example, will affect your emotional health, and vice versa. Nevertheless, the beauty of a holistic approach is that *any one step, appreciated and implemented, will eventually encompass all others.*

Bearing this in mind, let us briefly preview the steps we will take together to see just what lies ahead:

- Step 1 deals with facing our emotions: tears, fears, and laughter. I put this one first because many recuperating people are surprised to find that their emotions run strong, even if they may be over the initial shock of the crisis.
- Step 2 addresses the needs of the physical body for exercise, rest, and a proper environment to stimulate our natural healing tendencies.
- Step 3 covers the challenge of having so much time on your hands. I offer advice and suggestions for how to adjust to a new routine, how to live one day at a time, and how to make the most of your "spare" time.
- Step 4 treats the crucial topic of active participation in your own recuperation.
- Step 5 looks at the ways in which others, such as family and friends, can help or hinder your recuperation process.

- Step 6 deals with how this crisis might become an opportunity for you—if only for greater self-understanding.
- Step 7 discusses the role of your mind in healing. The power of thinking is greater than most of us care to admit. Working with this in mind, we may befriend a powerful ally.
- Step 8 concerns spiritual openings, such as gratitude and forgiveness, and touches on the deeper understanding of life, truth, and reality that recuperating people commonly glimpse after facing their crisis squarely.
- Step 9 enters the final phase of the recuperation process and suggests ways to ease your transition back into life.
- Step 10 reviews the previous steps and shows how they can be used as preventive medicine to create a healthier lifestyle from here on.

Each step presents ideas and suggestions for new ways to perceive your crisis, as well as specific activities to start immediately, such as breathing exercises, relaxation techniques, and so on. In many cases, several different activities might help you, but only one or two have been chosen so that you can get a taste of such healing strategies as you read on. Wherever appropriate, you will then be referred to the extensive set of appendices in this book for additional activities and exercises to pursue at your leisure.

Not all of what is presented will be necessary or practical for you. A few of the suggestions are old bromides—tried-and-true prescriptions about the nature of life and how to deal with crisis (the kind of wisdom *your* mother may have prescribed). Most of what is shared here, however, will be new for you and will perhaps challenge your customary thinking about health or illness. My own study and years of teaching in this field have convinced me that many valuable approaches to healing are often underemphasized, if not totally neglected, in the recovery programs that our doctors and hospitals may set out for us. I include many of these alternative approaches and trust that there is something here for everybody.

As you read, you may also wish to consider keeping a personal healing journal. In this journal you can capture your thoughts, feelings, and ideas in order to chart your progress as you recuperate. If you cannot write at this time, try speaking into a tape recorder. Keeping a journal allows you to reflect on issues that arise as you heal, to explore your creativity, and to release your feelings when there is no one around to share them with. You can also chart your progress, recording changes in physical ability, appetite, strength, and so on.

Throughout this book, you will encounter numerous questions to consider about your life and this period of recuperation. While you can always write your answers on the nearest scrap of paper, you are sure to find it more useful to keep your thoughts together in one place. If you want or need more information on how to keep a journal, see appendix A.

Before we begin, consider this Chinese folk tale that I have often related to people in crisis: An old man had a magnificent horse. The old man was poor, and this horse was not only his sole valuable possession but a dearly loved friend. One day the king of the region, passing the old man's property, spotted the gorgeous animal and immediately sent a messenger to offer a generous sum for the horse. But the old man refused, and his neighbors were appalled.

A week later the same prized horse vanished, leaving the old man with nothing. Hearing of the loss, his neighbors paid a visit and loudly lamented the situation. But the old man merely advised, "Do not say that it is good or bad; simply say that my beautiful horse is no longer in my yard." Looking at him in disbelief, the neighbors left, shaking their heads.

A fortnight passed, and one morning the old man looked out his window to see his faithful steed bounding across the plains, followed by three wild stallions and six mares. All ten horses found their way into his barn, so he ran out and barred the door.

Now his neighbors really had something to talk about. "How lucky you are," they cheered. But the old man would not be moved. "Do not say that it is good or bad," he repeated. "Whereas before I had no horse, now I have ten. That is all." Once again his neighbors thought him a sad and silly soul.

The following week as he was breaking the wild stallions, the old man's only son was thrown violently. His legs were badly broken, and the physicians predicted that he would always be lame. One would think that this was tragedy indeed. Yet the old man took it all in stride. "Do not say that it is good or bad. Simply say that my son was riding the horse, fell off, and now he is injured." And the neighbors, as before, were aghast.

Before the year was out a great war erupted in the kingdom, and all the young men of fighting age were conscripted. The army was poorly trained and suffered great losses. But because the old man's crippled son was never required to serve, he remained at home to support his aging father. As the news of battle casualties spread throughout the land, the old man's neighbors tried their best to get him to celebrate his good fortune in having his son spared. But he was not persuaded. "How do I know if this is good or bad," he humbly admitted, "when I know only such a small part of the great story of life?"

You really have no way of knowing what this health crisis will mean ultimately in your future life. The important thing is not to judge it or yourself right now. Rather, the important thing is to live it—as gently and responsibly as you can, and to do that moment . . . to moment . . . to moment. As they say, just take one step at a time.

❧

Allow Your Tears, Your Fears, and Your Laughter

> Not everything that is faced can be changed; but nothing can be changed until it is faced.
>
> JAMES BALDWIN

When my friend Jeff hurt his back in a bicycling accident, he was seriously depressed for weeks. Having to "lie low" was a shock to his active, independent spirit. Unable to fill up his days with work, he began to question his basic self-worth, to dwell on the unfulfilled dimensions of his life. He was overwhelmed by how strong his emotional reactions were; by the "tears and fears," as he called them.

Anita's story was similar. Her surgery was over and successful, from all the doctor's reports. Yet in the hospital she broke into sobs. "I don't even know why I'm crying," she whispered through her tears. "One minute I feel great, the next thing I know I'm curled up clutching my covers like a frightened child."

Ron was angry. First a terrifying heart attack, then triple-bypass surgery, followed by weeks of what he called "tentative living" and boredom. "This isn't what I signed up for," he spoke emphatically, his fist clenched on the table as we talked.

None of these responses is a surprise to me. Jeff, Anita, Ron, and perhaps you have lost something very precious and very personal—a sense of control, of being the prime movers in most aspects of life, a sense of invulnerability. The results of such losses are quite predictable. Tears, fears, anger—all are common at times like these. Jeff and Anita and Ron were each experiencing grief in their own way, just as you might be doing.

Grief is the normal, healthy, and necessary response to loss, and accidents and illnesses are filled with losses. We lose control. We lose our independence and the opportunity to participate in choices that were previously ours. We may lose job assignments, which can mean a loss of income. We also lose a certain sense of specialness that separates us from the rest of humanity. *Illness or serious injury happens to other people,* we unconsciously assume. *But now it has happened to me. I am one of the statistics—no longer the special, invulnerable person I imagined.*

Phil, whose left leg was seriously damaged in a motorcycle accident, put it like this: "It was a shock that was so great it caused my whole structure (physical, emotional, mental) to be upended. I lost the world in the way I had known it before my accident. All that I had built up about who I was—my self-definition or self-concept—was temporarily blown apart. In many ways I felt like a newborn infant—nearly helpless, and having to learn how to live. I lost my old self, and that wasn't easy to take. Believe me."

When something that we previously took for granted—or something that we held as rightfully ours—is suddenly wrenched from us, we grieve. Even when it is as minor as finding that our favorite TV show has been preempted by a special political report, a whole range of emotional reactions and unexpected behaviors may be triggered. We might yell at the TV for a few minutes to dispel our frustration. We might turn the TV dial to every other station and search the program guide in disbelief, muttering all the while, "This can't be," even when the evidence is right before us.

When we lose something major—a healthy heart, a breast, a friend or spouse, a job—we are really losing part of the definition of who we are, and we grieve all the more. Our grief will show up in physical ways, like disrupted sleep and change of appetite; in mental ways, like confusion and memory loss; and in emotional ways, like depression, anger, and sadness. Our grief is not one feeling or response, but rather a whole collage of reactions that can touch every aspect of our lives.

What have you lost as a result of this health crisis? Take a moment to write down your losses in your journal, or simply make a mental list of them. As you do, try to remember that it's okay to admit to losing, or to feeling a loss. This can be difficult, because losing is generally associated with failure of some kind. But it is not failure; it is just an aspect of being alive, of being human. Think about it!

STAGES OF GRIEF IN ILLNESS—IN BRIEF

Everybody grieves, because we all endure loss at some time in our lives. Knowing that your tears, fears, confusion, or anger are normal—as agonizing as they may be—can help alleviate your concern that you are crazy or alone in this. Learning to recognize the stages in the grieving-and-healing process may provide a larger framework on which to hang and understand your individual pain.

The renowned psychiatrist Elisabeth Kübler-Ross identified five stages in the mourning of a loss: denial, anger, bargaining, sadness, and acceptance. I have found her map of the territory to parallel the one that most recuperating people follow.

For simplicity, I prefer to divide the grieving-and-healing process into three phases: beginning, middle, and end. The beginning phase is characterized by shock and frequently some form of denial. In the middle phase, as healing progresses, come the emotions—the tears and fears, anger, panic, and confusion—as we begin to understand the full impact of our illness. With time, we move into the final phase of readjustment and reintegration into life as it is. Let's take a brief look at each of these phases to understand them better and to determine where you might be.

In the Beginning: Shock and Denial

It all starts with shock. For you it may have been a terrifying moment of chest pain, or discovering a lump that was never there before. The varieties of shock are infinite. Like the ringing of an alarm clock, it rouses us from sleep. Shock interrupts the expected flow of our lives; crisis doesn't make concessions to our important plans.

Shock is often accompanied by denial. "This can't be! I was only skiing a beginner slope," I cried as I lay in the emergency room after breaking my leg. Even after I admitted the break, I denied the seriousness of it by challenging the doctor: "You don't have to put a cast on my leg, just wrap it up like an athletic injury—besides, I'll heal myself in a few weeks."

Distorted thinking that holds little regard for the extent or implications of the injuries is a form of denial. Consider the case of Don. One evening after work he joined his buddies at a local pub. After one drink he became violently sick. He knew that something was seriously wrong. Yet, in what he jokes about now as his "last macho act," Don refused his friends' offers of help and set out to drive himself to the hospital. En route, he suffered a ruptured aortic aneurysm and crashed his car over an embankment. Months later, he spoke with remorse and humor about his "advanced degree of B.S.D. (Bachelor of Supreme Denial)."

Often, people deny the emotional impact that the crisis or trauma has had or is having on their lives. They keep up a smiling exterior, even acting in a flippant, joking manner about their condition. Meanwhile disrupted sleep, upset stomachs, headaches, or other stress symptoms tell a tale of something else entirely that is going on inside.

For some people, denial takes the form of numbness. Looking around at the world, everything seems a bit unreal, even absurd. "It was like the mind had gone on tilt," one woman described it. "I couldn't quite believe there was anything to be concerned about, because I literally felt nothing." Others withdraw into themselves when threatened.

Each of these denial strategies can be a valuable, even essential, survival mechanism. They allow you time to catch your breath; they give some necessary distance from the crisis situation. They may get you out of the way of further danger or injury. They may provide your system a chance to strengthen itself, to generate the energy needed for healing. As the truth slowly dawns on you, your body has time to establish some balance. You are adjusting, preparing yourself to deal with each new challenge presented by your accident or illness.

The Middle Stage: Anger and Panic

Not everybody acknowledges it, but anger in some form commonly follows denial. Anger is generally a positive sign—a welcome relief from the numbness. As frightening as it can sometimes be, anger catalyzes the healing process and provides us an outlet for the frustration, disbelief, and helplessness we may feel when confronted by a health crisis. As the shock begins to wear off and the truth can no longer be postponed, you may feel enraged, even if you don't express it. "Why me?" is the typical question at this point and "It's not fair!" the typical lament.

Following a car accident, Anna, at age nineteen, awoke in a

hospital bed and found herself in a body cast from toes to neck. She described her anger in vivid terms. "When I finally understood that I would have to remain this way for six months, a rage more violent than I had ever known started building within me. Soon I screamed. My *no* echoed throughout the long, lonely corridors of the hospital. I cursed; I pleaded with my attendants to release me, to cut me free from this plaster prison. My furious outbursts alarmed my helpers and friends. They alarmed me, too, but they helped in a funny sort of way. Sort of like screaming was my demand—for life."

It is also natural at this stage to experience panic and anxiety. You want to do something—anything—to make yourself feel better, to make this "bad dream" go away. Your helplessness to change what is can dredge up some deep, primitive responses. You may experience difficulties in breathing, as if there were a constriction in your chest or belly. You may find that you wake up feeling afraid; that little things will easily magnify into seemingly overwhelming obstacles; that worries about your present and future condition, the security of your family, your job, your life in general, seem to fill every corner of your mind, making it hard to think straight. And these powerful responses may be frightening if you have never felt them with such intensity before. But this too is normal.

No one ever told me that grief felt so like fear.

        C. S. LEWIS, *A Grief Observed*

Your anger may show itself in jealousy toward others, in resentment of their health or good fortune. People around you may seem gross and insensitive in the ways they take life for granted, when for you eating a meal or taking a bath may be a major undertaking. Nobody, it seems, really understands the extent of your pain or discomfort. *How dare the world go on as usual when I'm suffering!* you may find yourself feeling.

You may look around for something or someone to blame for your condition, for your confused or hurt feelings. It's natural to want a target for your anger—the guy in the other car, the doctor who didn't get to you on time, the mechanic who last adjusted the brakes, and most commonly yourself. *How could I be so stupid? I knew differently all along. Why didn't I do something about this sooner?* For some of us, God receives the brunt of our anger. We lash out against this supposedly loving Father or Mother who would allow a child to undergo such misery, who would seemingly desert us when our need is greatest. A sense that bad things shouldn't ever happen to good people—*What did I do to deserve this?*—is common.

Many recovering heart-attack patients report their "short-fuse" reactivity to things in general. If you are normally not a complainer but suddenly notice that the whole world is out to annoy you, this is only another of the many subtle ways that anger shows up. Your care givers will notice this change, even if you don't. Lori, who supported Phil after his accident, vividly remembers the day she came home from the store with a bag of red potatoes that she planned to cook for dinner. Phil took one look at the potatoes and flew into a tirade about how small they were, and how they were the "wrong kind." Anger gets triggered by whatever happens to be in the way when that emotional "last straw" is laid on our backs. There is often no connection between the importance of the event and the strength of the response. Anger doesn't need to make sense.

Sadness, confusion, and pain. Before, during, or after the anger, sadness will accompany your loss. Now you are facing more fully the extent of what is happening, and there is no longer any place to hide. You hurt. You may shed tears or sigh deeply and often. Or you might simply feel a big emptiness inside that nothing seems capable of filling. One man spoke of "an aching or longing sensation, but I don't know for what."

This sadness may not be confined to just the present health crisis and its implications. Painful memories of all sorts may rise unexpectedly. When I contracted hepatitis, I was alone in India. During the eight weeks I spent in bed there, I relived my whole life many times over. I cried for all the opportunities I had missed, for all the people I had ever hurt, for all the meanness and selfishness—little things—that I had done. I grieved for others, too—people in my situation, and especially those who I knew were much worse off, all over the world. Vulnerability has a way of inspiring compassion.

When you are recuperating, grieving some loss of independence, energy, or health, you may find that your thinking is confused or that you are more forgetful than usual. Memory loss is a frequent complaint of heart-surgery patients in particular. As one friend put it: "My accident turned my whole world on its head. Guess I shouldn't have been so surprised when things looked and felt a bit odd, overwhelming, or impossible to figure out." It's going to take some time for you to learn to see and cope and remember, with life so upside down.

Do try at this stage, and throughout the process, to keep in mind that everything changes. Slowly, as emotions surface and are acknowledged, as we talk out our pain and sense each texture of our loss, the seemingly bottomless pit starts to fill. Feelings that started out being razor-sharp get rounded over time. Instead of trying to avoid, deny, or repress our pain, we learn instead new ways to breathe *with it.*

The End: Readjustment and Reintegration

This final phase has it own unique challenges. As strength returns and bones and blood vessels mend, the prospect of "life as usual" may draw us forward with dreamy enthusiasm or else hang heavy over our heads. Now is the time that many people face the need for incorporating dramatic changes in lifestyle—dietary adjustments, giving up smoking or drinking, learning to use an artificial limb. Even if our readjustment is minor—temporary use of a cane, modified work schedule—emotions may be strained, mood swings may be wide, and self-esteem may continue to be questioned.

Hundreds of new opportunities are offered every day in which you can be reminded that life will go on, but it will never be quite the same as a result of your accident or illness. Each of these events must be integrated—that is, faced, felt, adjusted to, and finally let go—if you are to move ahead into the full experience of healing and wholeness. That is why it is called "grief work." It takes energy, patience, and courage for the body and mind and soul to complete the process. And that's what we'll do together as you work with this book.

Before moving on, reflect for a moment on which stage (beginning, middle, or end) best describes your overall process now. Keep in mind that these stages will always overlap one another.

Even from the final phase of readjustment you may experience waves of denial, as well as many feelings of anger and sadness. Consider the following story, which has sustained and guided many of us throughout the grieving-and-healing process:

An old king, tired of battling the emotional wars of life, publicized throughout the land his request. What he asked for was something that could make him happy when he felt sad, and sad when he felt happy. A wise man fashioned for him a ring on which a single sentence was engraved: THIS TOO SHALL PASS.

Remember that.

SPEAKING THE UNIVERSAL LANGUAGE: FEELINGS

Illness inclines most of us to be intensely emotional. Emotions are part and parcel of what it is to be a human being; they are a universal language of sorts. We may live on opposite sides of the globe, eat different foods, believe in different things, salute different flags, but when we are hurt, we feel pain. When we are healed, we feel joy.

I talk about this "permission to be human" in the college classes I teach in grief and loss, sometimes inviting a guest speaker to share openly with the group about his or her loss. The night that Sharon spent with us was particularly memorable.

"So what do you do when your worst-case scenario proves to be true?" Sharon faced my class quietly, not really expecting an answer. She simply watched the faces of students and felt the tears that rose in almost every eye. Sharon, twenty-nine years old, was attractive, professionally dressed, and energetic. She was also seated in a motorized wheelchair, paralyzed from her chest down as a result of an automobile accident ten years before. With great humor and candor she told us her story.

"It was Friday night, and I was coming home from a get-together with friends, other students at the university where I was in my sophomore year majoring in dance. Two drunk teenagers from town drove their car across the double yellow line and hit me, head on. I woke up to the nightmare of paralysis. Something this big is too much for anyone to comprehend all at once. It takes months, and in my case, years, for the full truth to be known and accepted. So what do you do in the meantime, besides think about suicide? I'll tell you what you do: You cry. You feel fear so big, so black and unending, that you're sure it will kill you if you let it get too close. You rage inside. And then you cry some more."

The room was silent. We held our breaths, too stunned to respond. But as Sharon continued her narration, our own tears and fears were triggered, and soon the silence was broken by a few sniffles, a few embarrassed sobs.

"It's okay to cry," Sharon consoled us. "We're all human here. We all feel stuff like this deeply. It's normal. And I'm here to tell you, and show you, that pain is okay too. And that the raw power of life is irrepressible!"

No one who met Sharon that night will ever forget these words. I've thought that they deserve to be printed out in bold letters and framed, hung on a wall for all to see and remember:

IT'S OKAY TO CRY

PAIN IS OKAY TOO

AND LIFE IS IRREPRESSIBLE!

It's Okay to Feel

Funny, isn't it, that we have to assure one another that it's "okay" to do something as simple and natural as shedding tears or admitting fears. No, it isn't funny, really, if you recognize that the emotional realm is not a logical place. Feelings are often irrational. Understanding them is often impossible. And the power that emotions release can be terrifying, especially if you're not used to such things.

Kate's story may give you some insight into this. Telling about her own illness, a complicated intestinal condition, she talked about her surprise discovery. "Before, I never thought I had fears," she said, smiling, "and would have vehemently defended the fact that I didn't—to anyone. For me, fears didn't exist. But then I found myself sick. I couldn't work. I could barely move. And that's when I felt them, thought about them, fought them—the fears. I'll tell you, it's intense to meet fears for the first time. Boy, was I naive! I guess I'd had them all along."

Perhaps you see yourself in Kate's story. This new experience of the "world turned upside down," which occurs with accident or illness, inspires in many people strong and strange reactions, great and powerful feelings and emotions. Perhaps you are experiencing unexpected waves of sadness, tears triggered by a song or a thought, outbursts of impatience, anger, rage at the sight of healthy people going about their lives. Even in the best of times, recognizing and expressing feelings in healthy ways can be a very big challenge. Dealing with them while you're also weak and hurting is an even bigger one.

However we learned them, we all carry around a host of mixed-up judgments about our feelings, like which ones are "good" for boys and which ones are "good" for girls. How many little boys were raised to "be tough," which translated into "Don't cry!" How many little girls were chastized for expressing anger? It's no wonder that as adults we have trouble with feelings.

Many of us make the unfortunate judgment that certain emotions such as fear, anger, jealousy, and pain are definitely "negative" and should therefore be rooted out. What will it take to convince ourselves that feelings themselves are neither good nor bad—they just are? In fact, painful feelings can be dynamic and positive in what they teach us and open us to receive.

For some people, the compulsion to run from feelings that we consider "bad" or negative is strong. But lying in bed or being limited in your energy and mobility offers no place to run to. If you can't keep busy you have to face your emotions. And that's a scary reality when your visitors are gone for the day and the TV has lost its charm, or when you're too weak to do anything but think.

Elisabeth Kübler-Ross, a pioneer in grief work, suggests that every hospital be equipped with a "scream room." This would be a private, sound-insulated place where a person could go to scream or cry as much as was necessary. In my frequent visits to hospitals, it has never ceased to amaze me that with all the pain people go through, both physical and emotional, I have rarely heard anyone cry and more rarely experienced someone expressing anger. How unfortunate that emotional release is not appreciated or encouraged by many doctors. What a sad commentary on our culture, which supposedly prizes physical and emotional health, that more direct ways of dealing with our emotion-filled bodies and minds aren't readily available.

Susan, a young woman who had recently suffered her second miscarriage in seven months, shared another aspect of this issue with me. Admitting that she constantly felt on the edge of tears, she was afraid to release them for fear that once she did the tears would never stop. "It's a bottomless pit," she told me. "I would never come out of it." I suggested that this simply wasn't true. "Letting go emotionally," I explained, "is very much like going for a good long run without a destination. When it is time to quit, the body will just naturally start to slow itself down. Even though there are times when you feel like you could go on forever, you don't. You'll stop. You can trust yourself this much." That's when she started to cry.

Remember in this process that *feelings are movements of energy passing through you.* They are generated by your thoughts, but they are not right or wrong, and are certainly not the totality of who you are. Similar to the way in which you watch an exciting movie, you can develop the ability to observe the shadows created by your feelings without identifying completely with them. You can watch from a distance, allowing the shadows to dance, without getting caught up in the dance yourself. You can also turn on the light— with your choice to move ahead despite the fears—when your fascination with the shadows has passed.

Allowing your feelings to be there and expressing them—or not, as appropriate—is perhaps the single most helpful action you can engage in right now. Remember that allowing feelings doesn't mean forcing them; it means acknowledging them. We create a whole lot more fear and pain for ourselves by trying to avoid our fear and pain. Running from it, we feed it. Denying it, we enrage it. Fear, anger, sadness, and rage are normal accompaniments to recuperation. Let yourself feel them. As Sharon reminded my students: "We're all human here. We all feel this stuff very deeply." Human beings are allowed to hurt!

Take a moment right now to acknowledge whatever feelings are moving through you at this time. Do you feel sadness? Anger? Loneliness? Fear? Or maybe even joy? Do you feel confused? Numb? Anxious? Grateful? Imagine embarking on an emotional inventory on yourself. Just allow the feelings to be there, without any pressure to express them in any particular way; without any necessity to do anything about them, unless you want to. Notice if you are holding your breath, or else breathing very shallowly as you do this. If so, simply allow yourself to take a fuller breath.

If you are having difficulty identifying your feelings, consult the list in appendix B, which outlines common emotions and reactions you may recognize as your own.

Fall Apart—and Fall Together

accident have a way of shattering more than limbs and
ecuperation is a time of shattered illusions of invulnera-
dependence, indispensability. But shattered illusions
often allow for reality to emerge in all its richness, ripeness, and
possibility. There is a chance for genuine healing, not just the
amelioration of symptoms or the mending of a bone or blood
vessel.

Recall for a moment that "healing" derives from the root
"whole." The healing into wholeness, which is the gift and opportunity of recuperation, is a healing of body, mind, spirit, emotions.
Celebrate whatever it takes to effect wholeness, even if that means
pain.

Falling apart is often a prelude to a falling together at a whole
new level of organization. My friend Meredith's transformation
attests to healing that is wholeness. I always thought of Meredith
as an irrepressible optimist. But she called me one day last summer
with a very sober tone in her voice that I had never heard before.
Softly, almost pleadingly, she asked if we could get together.

The woman who greeted me was not the Meredith I had
known. Her always trim, athletic body looked gaunt and tired. She
had lost quite a bit of weight and there was a grayness about her
eyes. She was in pain, despite the brave smile that tried to reassure
me. She looked like a person who had seen a ghost.

As we talked, Meredith recounted a story I had heard before,
a story of collapse of the seemingly solid foundations of her life.
A back operation had confined her to bed for several weeks and
kept her at home for several more. The surgery was major but the
prognosis for complete recovery was good. So why wasn't she
springing back to life as usual, as she had always done before with
any setback?

"The frightening part," she whispered as if fearful that someone else might hear the sorry truth, "is that I have never felt so
helpless before. This is not the me I knew." I asked her to elaborate.

"I had no idea that sadness could be a concrete overcoat,
weighing me down so badly that I literally couldn't move. Or that
fear—fear of losing work, fear of losing my spouse, fear of being
dependent, fear of being sick, fear of fear—could make my chest
so tight that it was difficult to breathe, or make me so weak and sick

to my stomach that I couldn't eat for days at a time. I feel like a stranger in the world. I feel lost and overwhelmed and confused. And I'm most afraid that this will never end."

"You're probably trying every technique in your bag of tricks, and all to no avail," I offered.

"You're right," she answered, surprised that I seemed to know. "I try to meditate, I force myself to take vitamins, and when that doesn't make me feel better I try deep breathing and praying and, well, you name it. I'm getting the feeling that I'm just not in control anymore, and that's something I've never experienced before."

That's when I said, "Congratulations!" to my friend, who looked at me in amazement. "As cruel as that sounds, I am rejoicing for you." As Meredith remained speechless, I continued. "I don't celebrate your pain; I know that it is terrible. But I do celebrate your falling apart, your realization of helplessness, and the depth of yourself you are getting to see and explore through all of this."

She began to breathe more deeply, and she listened because she knew that I had lived through similar breakdowns, and here I was stronger and healthier on the other side.

When we parted less than an hour later, relief was evident in her face and all over her body. Where before there was only disorientation, there was now one tiny shred of assurance. "There is a beginning, a middle, and an end to what you are going through," I told her firmly. "And you will survive. And someday you'll even remind someone else the way I'm reminding you."

Meredith phoned about two months later to tell me that the worst was over. "Our meeting was a turning point for me," she said with strength, softened by the wisdom she was acquiring. "I have opened so many new, painful doors inside myself. But these openings into feelings, fearful thoughts, and emotions have broadened and deepened my appreciation for life, as well as my compassion for myself and others. I am being healed in ways I never imagined possible. While I don't enjoy the pain and hope it's all over soon, I *have* benefited from it."

Moved by her words, I expressed gratitude to those who had been there for me when I was "falling apart" in a similar way. Over the years I have come to see that falling apart is a gift to be opened. My friend Dean spoke about it this way: "When I hug the shadow that has frightened me, I turn it into a valued friend."

It's Okay to Feel Good—and Laugh, Too!

Not all the emotions people encounter during recuperation are disagreeable. It is quite possible to feel remarkably good and even to enjoy periods of genuine happiness despite your condition. Perhaps the peak of your crisis has passed and you are coasting down the other side just grateful to be alive. I was often reluctant to admit how good I felt and what a great time I sometimes had when I was sick, even with the pain and discomfort. It can be lovely to be taken care of, to get special attention. And joy is not limited by particular circumstances. Often it surprises us at the most unexpected times. Life *is* irrepressible. Joy is one of the most powerful prescriptions available for encouraging the healing process.

Democritus, that sweet old Greek who discovered atoms, wasn't just whistling "Dixie" when he said that the main task of human intelligence is to take life, which is presented to us as tragedy, and transform it into comedy.

MURRAY KORNGOLD,
The Holistic Health Lifebook

Norman Cousins, the man who assisted his own healing from a life-threatening disease by a regimen of vitamins and laughter, knew from his study of classic books on stress that disease was encouraged by the chemical changes in the body produced by a steady diet of anger and fear. He wagered a bet with himself that the opposite effects could be achieved by focusing more consciously on such life-enhancing emotions as hope and love, and by mixing everything with laughter.

Cousins found that short periods of hearty laughter were enough to induce several hours of painless sleep. He read humorous stories and joke books; he laughed. He watched Marx Brothers movies and "Candid Camera" TV sequences and laughed some more. Slowly and steadily he began to regain control of his body and to move without excruciating pain.

Years later he worked with others to encourage the same effect. He tells of an experiment with a group of patients at a VA hospital. Playing a cassette tape recording of nothing but laughter, Cousins watched as the contagion spread throughout his audience. "They were on a runaway laughter course and couldn't stop. Some of them couldn't stay in their chairs . . . I was rolling along with the rest." After ten minutes, when the laughter finally subsided, some of the patients reported that their pain had actually receded. And the energy of the entire room had changed dramatically.

Laughter and simple good humor are antidotes to pain because they interrupt the worry cycle—the obsession with a problem that leads to a buildup of tension, resulting in increased pain, which further increases concern about the problem, which in turn kicks the cycle in all over again at a higher level of intensity. Anything that helps to break this deadly serious occurrence, which Cousins calls the "panic cycle," will assist you in short-circuiting its normal outcome.

An ancient Buddhist meditation technique is recommended to this end. Immediately upon arising, jump out of bed and start moving your body in the most ridiculous postures you can create. Meanwhile, make silly faces and force yourself to make sounds like laughing. Ha, ha, ho, ho, hee, hee . . . whatever. And while there may be a deep, esoteric significance to this practice, the practical result is that it makes you start the day with a smile. Just putting a grin on your face and simulating the experience of laughter actually causes a chemical reaction in the brain that leads to a sensation of pleasure.

Researchers today are finding that laughter stimulates the production of endorphins and enkephalins, powerful chemical pain relievers in the brain. Furthermore, laughing pumps adrenaline and other hormones into the bloodstream, thus charging the heart and lungs. As your laughter continues, the heart beats faster, arteries contract, and blood pressure temporarily rises. The blood receives more than its usual dosage of oxygen (a healthy addition for most of us, who breathe very poorly most of the time), and immune-cell production increases.

Laughter serves the function of an internal massage—"internal jogging," Cousins calls it. In an average laugh you will work the diaphragm, thorax, abdomen, heart, and even the liver, to say nothing of your facial muscles. And when you stop laughing and your arteries and muscles relax, your blood pressure is reduced. Such a process can aid digestion, take the natural form of a sleeping pill or laxative, and even burn a few extra calories along the way.

Try this experiment yourself. Just start laughing—out loud. Don't stop, no matter how foolish you feel. Don't be half-hearted in your laughter either. Laugh as vigorously as you possibly can. Laugh louder than you dare. And keep it up for at least five full minutes. That's a long time, so don't give up too soon. Are you ready? Perhaps you want to warn the people around you first—but better yet, surprise them and invite them to laugh with you. Get set. Now go! *Laugh.*

Humor is available everywhere once you start listening or looking for it. Books of jokes or cartoons, movies, audio tapes, songs, friends who are just naturally humorous—use them all, especially when the tears and fears get overwhelming. Sometimes a phone call or a simple request is all that's required: "Hello, Mike? I'm pretty low now and need something—anything—to remind me to laugh again." Or just ask for a mirror and start making faces at yourself. Above all, keep in mind the amusing morsels we and others continually come across.

Otis Bowen, the secretary of health and human services during the Reagan administration, was a small-town doctor for over thirty years. Here's one of the stories he loved to tell about himself and his former patients: A physician in the pediatric ward overhears a conversation. One boy asks another whether he's in the hospital for "medical or surgical reasons." The second lad looks puzzled, so he tries putting it another way: "What I mean is, were you sick when you came in or did they make you sick after you got here?"

Then there's the one about Ronald Reagan himself, who, having been shot and rushed to George Washington University Hospital, turned to his surgeons as they entered the operating room and remarked, "Please tell me you're Republicans."

Speaking of hospitals, one of my favorites was told in a Woody Allen movie. Two old women, who love to spend their time complaining about everything, are having dinner together in the nursing home. Just as their plates are set in front of them one old woman turns to her friend and bemoans, "Agh, but the food in this place is terrible." To which her friend responds, "Yes, and such small portions!"

Remember, there are times when laughter will be your best medicine, and other times when you need to cry and should. There will be times for keeping a tight control and times for releasing that control. As the Book of Ecclesiastes in the Bible says: "To everything there is a season, and a time to every purpose under heaven." The fine art of recuperation is a commonsense process. Listen to what your own process is asking from you, and at the same time don't be afraid to try something new if it seems appropriate.

FIRST AID FOR FEELINGS

Some feelings are so powerful that they can easily make a bright day gray. When you are flat on your back in bed or weakened by a health crisis, your feelings and thoughts about even a minor problem may take the form of gigantic shadows lurking around your bed, awaiting you at every turn. Unchecked, worries have a tendency to grow out of proportion. When that happens you can apply some first-aid procedures, helpful ways to regain a more balanced perspective.

Following are eight practical suggestions for loosening yourself from the grip of strong emotions:

Invite support in facing your feelings. You may find it helpful to talk out your concerns with friends or care givers. Your best friends are the ones who will give you the benefit of their balanced perspective, their honesty, and their compassion. You may need that, since yours may be askew right now.

Remember that illness and pain tend to encourage isolation. It is natural to try to keep control, to avoid burdening others, and especially to feel humiliated in admitting to emotional unsteadiness. So often in my life I fell into the trap of believing I was the only one who had ever had such a problem. The longer I kept my pain private, the more painful it became.

Margaret, a beautiful woman in her early forties, perfectly exemplifies this tendency: "For years I carried around a fear of getting cancer, despite my apparent good health. I was too embarrassed to speak about it, since I was sure that I was the only woman in my circle of friends who ever harbored such thoughts. So I kept my secret carefully guarded. One day when several of us were sharing health concerns, I was amazed to hear another 'healthy' woman talk about her cancerphobia. What a shock. I just looked at her and gasped, 'You too?' It was such a relief to finally have permission to talk about this. It was the beginning of a process of healing. Recently I found an incredible message in a Chinese fortune cookie: 'You think it's a secret, but everybody knows.' I would put it this way: 'You think you're the only one, but you are not alone.' "

Here again, talking out this dilemma with others is extremely valuable. It's only necessary to start: "Hey, friend, I don't know what I'm feeling—I'm just not feeling good . . ." and the shadows are exposed to the light.

Breathe. I sat with Kris for about two hours one afternoon shortly after he left the hospital. His abdomen was laced with stitches, and he reported feeling anxious and sad. The longer we talked, the more tired I became. I could hardly keep from yawning every minute or so. I began to feel anxious too.

Then I realized what was happening. I hadn't taken a deep breath in almost half an hour. I was breathing sympathetically with Kris, and he was breathing as shallowly as possible to avoid stretching his scarred belly.

"Kris," I said, "we're not really breathing." We both paused, inhaled slowly, then exhaled. "Oh, that feels so good," he remarked. "Please stay around and remind me to breathe more. I had deliberately forgotten."

Whatever it was that sent you to bed, you're going to have to keep breathing if you ever want to get out. That's obvious. But not so obvious is the connection between emotional states and respiration. Strong feelings, especially painful ones, can just "knock the wind out of you." For example, recall a time when you narrowly missed hitting another car or an object. Your heart was pounding; you may have felt weak and drained. Your breathing became shallow, and you may have tried to take a deep breath to help yourself balance out.

In fact, nothing hurt you in this incident. There was no impact. But your emotional state of fear or anger triggered a whole range of physical responses that left you feeling as if you had been hit by something. In respiration as well as other processes, the mind-body connection is strong. Your mind registers danger, your emotions flare in response, and your body feels the effects. Just by observing the breathing process, most people find they can slow it down and deepen it, and that creates overall relaxation. And this is valuable first aid for panic feelings, too.

Try this breathing exercise now. Inhale through your nose, expanding your abdomen so that it fills up and out like a balloon. Hold the breath for a count of three, and now exhale through your mouth, allowing the air to make the voiceless sound "hu" as it passes over your lips and teeth. Imagine that the expelled air leaves your mouth in a thin stream, rather than in one big puff. Now inhale through your nose, expand the belly, and hold and release again, in the same way. Do this two or three more times. Rest, and simply observe what, if anything, has changed about your breathing as a result. Do you feel any better?

Here is another breathing exercise: Focus your eyes on the most soothing sight in your immediate environment and keep them there. Breathe deeply and don't stop. Mentally repeat: "1,000, 2,000, 3,000, 4,000" as you inhale through your nose. Exhale from your mouth, mentally counting: "1,000, 2,000, 3,000, 4,000." Keep breathing this way for a full five minutes.

Now tense every muscle in your body as tightly as you can. Tense your face; clench your fists and toes, if possible. Hold this for a count of ten. Then slowly release this tension. Now breathe again deeply. Stop thinking and take a rest.

Finally, make a sound such as "ba" or "da" as loudly as you can. Feel the reverberation of the sounds in your body. Keep making the sound until you feel relaxed. Then repeat this phrase to yourself: "I am here, I'm alive, I can cope, I survive."

Many additional breathing exercises can be found in appendix C. Use them now or refer to them when you need them.

Be easy on yourself. Loosely translated, this means "get off your own case"—if only for a few hours. There is a tendency, especially when you start reading self-help books (like this one), to try to incorporate everything that you hear or read about all at once. Not only is this an impossible task, but it can be downright detrimental. Demanding change can be self-defeating; it can also create a tremendous amount of guilt and tension.

Merely *understanding* that something is good for you or *remembering* what you know you should do doesn't ensure that you'll be able to put that understanding to work in your body right away. And it certainly won't change your thinking patterns overnight.

In *Dreaming the Dark,* author Starhawk describes two voices that "speak" to us inside our own head. One is the voice of the self-hater who demands, criticizes, judges everything, and finds us wanting. It challenges us to *do something* right away. The other voice is that of the guardian—really the voice of reason, the voice of balance, the voice of God. This voice speaks of what is necessary for healing in practical terms. It supports and encourages but doesn't coddle. It suggests instead the gentle path of patience and self-acceptance, of one step at a time.

The easiest way to make immediate use of your guardian is to imagine that you are advising someone else in your exact situation. What would you tell your best friend to do if she felt the way you felt and was being demanding toward herself besides? What would you say if he had gone through the accident or surgery or illness that you had and needed some emotional support right now? There you have it. Take your own advice. Be easy on yourself, and listen to your own "guardian" angel.

Let it go by yelling. You may have learned by now that certain behaviors are expected of "good patients," and that strong emotions that rock the boat of normal routine are not among them. You may fear emotional release because it will upset those around you, and you may be right. Those who have never done it themselves may feel threatened. They may fear that you are getting worse, when more likely the opposite is true. Your emotional expression may simply be triggering their own tears and fears. But don't let that stop you. There are lots of "safe" ways to let yourself go that won't get you labeled for life and that also will keep you in touch with a sense of control in the process.

Years ago I learned a technique called the silent scream, in which I "let myself go" for only ten minutes at a time, and without making a sound. Try it when you are alone or in the company of someone you trust. Open your mouth and let loose with your breath, your facial contortions, your vigorous body movements. For me, an unvocalized scream or cry or even laughter works every bit as effectively as a vocalized one. Try it. Or try screaming into a pillow. Allow ten minutes for the process, no more. When the time is up, just stop and turn your attention to something else, or snuggle up with your teddy bear if you have one, and take a nap.

These are just two of many proven strategies to cope with anger. Additional safe alternatives are contained in appendix B.

Learn to relax. But don't try to force it. That's about as helpful as trying to force yourself to fall asleep. One way to release yourself, temporarily, from the grip of fear, anxiety, and sadness is to let painful feelings out by the back door. In other words, "trick yourself" into relaxation by simply directing your attention, gently, toward something else.

The following stress reliever works for almost everyone. I call it the "slump." In whatever position your body is now, let it slump—that is, let it drop or sink into whatever you are lying on or sitting on. Surrender your weight to your bed or chair. Drop your head forward; let your neck support it. If your condition doesn't allow this movement, you can still slump in your own way. Let your face slump. Stop trying to hold a smile or keep your eyes wide open. Let your buttocks slump; release the tightness there. Let your belly slump; no need to hold on to it. Realize that all parts of you can be supported without trying so hard.

Pretend that you are a rag doll. If someone were to try to lift your arm, it would drop like a deadweight. Now focus on your right arm alone and say to yourself: "My right arm is heavy, my right arm is heavy . . ." Say this over and over slowly for at least twenty seconds as you continue to concentrate on your right arm from the fingertips all the way up to your armpit. "Feel" your arm grow heavy. After the twenty seconds are up, make a fist and flex your arm and fingers as much as possible. Take a deep breath and open your eyes if they have been closed.

How do you feel? What you have learned is part of a relaxation program called *autogenic* training. As you train yourself to make your right arm heavy, you will move on to your left arm, then to your legs. Soon you will be able to extend this heaviness and the accompanying relaxation to your whole body, from head to toe. Appendix C contains several other techniques for relaxation.

Let the music play! Dr. Richard Moss, who uses music as a significant part of his healing work with clients, asserts that "music can activate energy centers, free areas of repressed energy, induce spontaneous reverie and imagery, and, in general, create a space to let go of control and expand boundaries."

You probably already know that music is a powerful evoker of mood and that certain pieces of music can trigger memories of events that leave us feeling ecstatic or sad. Let music assist you in allowing the tears, the fears, the joy, the laughter. Use it for "getting down" or "soaring up," as appropriate. Listen to great music, classical music, or music composed specifically to encourage relaxation and healing, of which there is much available today. Listen to the music with more than your ears. Let music penetrate your heart, clear out your brain, energize your lungs.

Try this right now. Ask a friend to put on some gentle music for you, if you can't do it for yourself. Close your eyes and breathe deeply and slowly as you imagine letting and feeling the music wash or flow over you. Realize that every cell in your skin is a vibrating membrane and will therefore be touched by the music. Imagine listening with every part of your body.

Sing or hum. Like laughter or a silent scream, singing can be a dynamic mood-altering activity. To "whistle a happy tune" or "sing a joyful song" may sound trite or naive. But the effects on the brain chemistry and the reduction of stress levels that this brings about are not insignificant. Often, the difference between feeling low or feeling high may be only a chorus away. I mean it. It is hard to maintain a serious attitude toward the world and your pain and problems when you are laughing or singing uproariously.

As you sing you need to breathe more fully, so it can be a fine form of exercise for someone who can't move around too much. Quite frequently as you sing you'll find that your toes and fingers will catch the beat and start moving too. Try this: Open your mouth wide and sing one word, any word—say, butterfly, or cantalope, or lollipop. Sing it "big" enough so that it reaches into every corner of your room. Make sure it fills the space under your bed. Keep singing until you know that your sound has touched everything in the room and set it all vibrating. As you sing your one word, allow it to evolve into a short phrase or sentence if you want to. It doesn't need to make sense. Sing words only because they sound good together. Laugh at yourself if you start to feel foolish, or laugh at me for suggesting such nonsense—either way, keep on singing. Think of it as your medicine. Why not compose the "Recuperation Theme" song—and when you've mastered it, send a copy along to me.

Remember the inscription "This too shall pass" on the wise king's ring? Why not make up a tune for this phrase and chant it, either out loud or silently, during times of stress and discouragement. Reinforce your remembrance by writing this phrase on a card and posting it near your bed or in a place where you will see it many times a day. Each time you look at it, let it remind you to breathe, to relax a bit, and to settle into the natural rhythm of healing that your body will assume if you let it.

Do something old, add something new. Experienced "bed-liers" will tell you that adding a spot of color or aliveness to yourself or your immediate environment will go a long way in helping to brighten your spirits. Use green plants or other living things—a bird in a cage, an aquarium of fish. Try varying the light in the room by removing curtains or changing light bulbs. Ask a friend to hang a new poster or picture on your wall. The possibilities are endless.

If you are in the hospital or other alien surroundings, something old and familiar—something that looks and feels like home—will be a welcome emotional support. Your own pajamas or nightgown; your own pillow and bedspread; those family photos; your coffee mug; your teddy bear. Ask friends or family to help make your environment a place of healing, not just enduring. Such small changes will make a tremendous difference in your ability to sustain the emotional ups and downs that life delivers at this time. The next chapter will offer you many more practical, simple suggestions.

Appreciate the Body in Bed

> Our body will take care of us if given
> the slightest chance. It already has the
> best of nature within it and will sur-
> vive if we will only let it, if we give it
> just half the chance it has given and
> continues to give us each day.
> RONALD J. GLASSER,
> *The Body Is the Hero*

"I hardly ever thought of my body before this happened," Sid confessed with embarrassment. Two months had passed since he had left the hospital after undergoing a double bypass. "Now I'm terrified of my body. It seems to have a mind of its own. It does bad things to me. It causes me pain. It seems to want to punish me for my neglect. I hate my body when it doesn't work right. I'm scared of what it will do next!"

Sid's response is a common one. There is nothing like a physical breakdown of any kind for waking you up to the truth that you have a body. Sick people are generally much more aware of their bodies than are healthy people, and understandably so. Illness has a way of motivating respect for the simplest bodily processes previously taken for granted.

It is common to notice every little pain, every nerve twitch, every gas bubble. It is even more common to assign meaning to them: "Oh, no, I'm getting worse." Or, "The disease is spreading." You've probably forgotten that when you were well you had twinges of pain, contractions, gas, and all sorts of similar inconveniences all the time. But your illness has narrowed your world considerably. The focus of your attention has changed from "out there" to "in here," and that's natural.

24

When you are sick it is convenient to have something to blame for the pain and inconvenience, and your body becomes a likely candidate. It becomes the enemy. It's easy to hate a bum leg, an aching back, a "worn-out ticker" and to add insult to injury by trying to dissociate from your body, forgetting that this flesh and blood and muscle and bone is *you.*

Listen to your own internal conversations about your body. Is there self-hatred, fear, confusion? Are you speaking about some "thing" as if it were outside of yourself? Consider the following story and its message about the body:

Once upon a time, a foolish man received an inheritance, a castle full of priceless treasures. But nobody gave him the key. So he moved into the cow shed, looking at his beautiful home, wondering about its riches. When his neighbors came to visit he entertained them by taking a ladder, leaning it against the wall of the castle under a window, and inviting his guests to climb up and take a look inside. Then they would retire to the shed to have tea and talk about the wonders they had seen.

After telling this story to a group of students one day, we explored the subject of healing. Laura, a woman in her late forties, wrote the following:

> I recognized myself in this foolish man. My body is a castle full of priceless treasures, but I so rarely inhabit it as if I owned it. Instead, I tend to live outside myself, looking in. I look at myself through the eyes of other people, and generally find that I'm not measuring up. I talk about my body as if it were separate from my mind, my heart, my soul. I use drugs or food to avoid my pain and to dull the intensity of my pleasure. I ask for other people's advice about how to change and repair something, but I rarely ever take a good look at the situation for myself.
>
> It's scary to ask for the key to yourself. I don't blame that foolish man. Moving into my body means that I'd have to take more responsibility.
>
> I'm not sure that I'm ready.

Even though we often obsess about our bodies as if that is all there were to us, we still speak and act as if the body were some separate entity, a machine from which we expect unquestioning service. Often, our only concern for the body emerges when it isn't doing its job right or when it isn't looking right. Many of us live out our entire lives without ever inquiring about the body—the key that would open us to a deeper understanding of ourselves.

The human body is, in fact, a castle filled with treasures. It is a miracle, remarkably forgiving and incredibly resilient, that will engage in unbelievably complex procedures to keep itself in balance. It has over 3 million years of experience to back it up. Most good doctors will tell you that they don't "cure" anything; they simply set up the ideal conditions so that the body/being can cure itself. So our job becomes clearer: to recognize and appreciate and honor this innate healing capacity of the human body.

Picking up the key and moving back in, to our bodies and ourselves, is an ideal way to start. Welcome home!

THE HERO IN THE BODY

Jerry was watching an educational-TV special about the human body. He was fascinated, even awestruck. Yet as he watched it he started to feel a bit anxious. "I began to think that I'd better understand all this stuff or I wouldn't be able to keep it going. And I knew I couldn't do it. All those incredible connections! It was too much for me." Although he laughed as he related this incident to me, we both still appreciated the feeling. "Thank God," he said, "we don't have to consciously control the whole process. We wouldn't have time to breathe, even if we did remember to." Jerry is right.

The "incredible connections" the body knows how to make are awesome. Its intelligence and adaptability are truly remarkable. Take the immune system, for example. When disease enters the body or unfriendly cells start gathering, your immune system is immediately activated. Wandering sentinels, white blood cells called *phagocytes* and their larger partners *macrophages,* begin amassing in great number around the invader agents, actually scooping up and ingesting infectious bacteria, destroying them on the spot in many cases—and being destroyed themselves. The pus that forms in an infected area is really the remains of battle, dead white cells and dead bacteria together.

The second line of defense is offered by the chemical substances present in the blood that neutralize bacterial poisons and destroy bacteria. These substances are called antitoxins and antibodies. Amazingly, each one is uniquely designed to counteract the effects of one particular type of virus, fungus, or bacteria.

The answer to how this "custom-design" process is engineered, how the right antibody appears at the right time, lies in the lymph system. Here another class of wandering white cells, called lymphocytes, act like data collectors in the body. As soon as any patrolling lymphocyte encounters a cell that fails to meet its standards of friendly behavior, it leaves the area and travels to a lymph node—its antibody factory—where, carrying the telltale data of the foreign invader, it transforms itself into a plasma cell and begins manufacturing the antibody proteins. These antibodies are then poured into the bloodstream as quickly as they are formed and head straight for the site of the invasion. Here they help draw together and assemble a complex of nine different protein molecules, serving much like a powerful rifle to blast a hole through the enemy cell wall. Outside fluids are now allowed to flow in. The enemy cell swells up and bursts.

This description is admittedly crude, but it will serve, I hope, to increase your respect for yourself. And realize: All of this goes on without your having to think about it!

A part of this story, however, does require some thinking. Mounting evidence indicates that the immune system can be weakened or veer off course when the body is overstressed for a long period of time. Understanding the connection between stress and the health of the body is basic.

The Body under Stress

Recuperation is supposed to be a time of relaxing and resting the body. Right? That is what it is *supposed* to be. Yet for many of us it turns into nearly the opposite. The shock of the health crisis, surgery, or physical therapy, the change of routine, the financial burden, the alteration of schedules and food, the introduction of drugs into the bloodstream, a reevaluation of priorities . . . the list of potentially stressful factors goes on and on. For some people the changes brought about by their condition are actually more difficult to bear than the health problem itself.

Yet some seem able to ride almost any wave with ease, while for others even a minor disturbance sets off alarm reactivity. Why? And what does this ability to adjust to change, to handle stress, have to do with recuperation? Let's take a look at the nature of stress and see what it does to the body.

Quite simply, stress is anything that taxes the human organism beyond its ability to immediately adjust. It may come from a physiological source, like a case of the flu that puts the immune system to work overtime and leaves us feeling drained of energy. It might have its roots in a psychological factor, like hearing that we've won the lottery, which may trigger such an adrenaline "rush" that we need to sit down to keep from falling over.

Both positive and negative life events require adjustment within the system. If the body can't balance itself out quickly enough, stress will be felt. Stress can be observed in behavior or attitude change, as well as in a whole range of physical reactions: alteration of blood chemistry, change in respiration and heart rate, sweating palms or chills among them.

It is important to realize that these reactions are not cause for concern. Actually, they are cause for gratitude. They testify to the fact that your body has a remarkable self-regulating environment that engineers these responses in an attempt to keep the original stressor from getting out of hand.

Take a common example. A person in an accident often reports feeling cold, even in very warm weather. (Perhaps you have experienced this yourself.) This is because the body, when threatened or stressed, withdraws energy from places that don't need it in order to reinforce the places that do. So if it isn't necessary for survival, the blood leaves the extremities and rushes to the vital organs of the body where extra protection is required. This sudden change can leave a person feeling cold, and for good reason. That's why you get a blanket for a person in shock.

Homeostasis is the technical term for this natural energy-balancing act. The body wants to survive; that is its first and most powerful instinct. A stressed body will respond in whatever ways are most appropriate to ensure survival. Sometimes that survival instinct will create temporary loss of consciousness, perhaps because the pain is too much to bear. At another time survival will mean "supercharged" reflexes, strength that we never thought possible available to help us avoid a catastrophe—as in when a slight woman lifts an automobile to release a trapped child. This is the "fight or flight" mechanism—a response that swings the body into high gear so that it may confront a threat or repair its injuries. Chances are that from the onset of your illness or accident, this great balancing act has been enacted over and over with each new or potentially disruptive event.

Biochemically what is happening is this: The perception of a threat (a stressful event) travels along nerve pathways to your brain where the alert is registered in your hypothalamus. From here a hormone is secreted sending messages to the adrenal glands (located on top of your kidneys) and to the pituitary gland (located at the base of the brain). In the adrenal glands are manufactured powerful neurochemicals that prime the body for action by increasing heart rate, breathing, alertness, and muscle response. The pituitary gland secretes a hormone that signals the release of cortisol into the bloodstream, further speeding up the body metabolism while at the same time causing a near shutdown of the digestive system. Thus reinforced, you are ready to wage war, so to speak—to fight or to flee.

Great system! But not inexhaustible. When this *general adaptation syndrome* (as Hans Selye, the father of stress research, named it) is overused, it wears itself out. The side effects of such a burnout are that vital organs, stimulated too hard and for too long, may break down. So a person with a weak heart who continues to stress it by poor diet or smoking, for instance, may eventually experience the consequences of such behavior with a worsening of the original condition. Growing evidence links stress with a wide range of disorders and diseases—high blood-pressure, kidney disease, peptic ulcer, endocrine gland disorders, skin disorders such as psoriasis, and diseases like rheumatic fever and rheumatoid arthritis.

One of the most devastating effects of chronic stress may be the suppression of the body's immune system. For thousands of years, physicians have known that people under stress (although they didn't use that word) were more susceptible to disease than those who were not. Certainly stress does not cause infection—for that a virus or fungus or bacterium must be present. But stress does lower the body's resistance to foreign invaders. Recent technological advances in medicine have allowed us access to the inner workings of the body and brain, verifying that the immune system is indeed linked to other physical systems and influenced by psychological events. One study of medical students during stressful examination periods revealed lower than normal antibody levels in the blood, indicating a greater vulnerability to infection. And for our purposes in recuperation, this is of vital concern.

A health crisis, like an accident or surgery or other major illness, ranks high on a list of life-stress events. In a famous study conducted during the 1960s by Thomas Holmes and Richard

Rahe, illness or personal injury was listed as the sixth highest cause of stress, preceded in intensity only by death of a spouse, divorce, separation, a jail term, and death of another close family member. The higher the ranking, the more energy or work it took (as in the grief work we spoke of in step 1) to reestablish a state of balance.

The body is an energy-conservation system. If the inner environment requires massive energy supplies (as yours does for the healing and balancing process), that means that less will be available for other things, like going back to your job or keeping up with your housework. So you need to rest to keep yourself balanced. The body is also an energy-transformation system. It needs appropriate energy supplies in the form of air, food, light, and so on in order that it may repair and nourish itself. So you need to eat well, to breathe well, and to get fresh air and sunlight whenever possible to support the healing that is taking place. Without proper rest and adequate raw materials for nourishment, the body is stressed and its ability to do its healing job is weakened.

But not everybody succumbs to the negative consequences of an overstressed system. Why? It seems that some people naturally handle stress better than others, and some people are able to neutralize the negative consequences by the use of stress-management techniques. An eight-year study at the University of Chicago dealing with managers at the telephone company revealed that those with a sense of being able to control work situations, along with those who felt stimulated by their work, were able to thrive, despite stress in their lives. In a Harvard Medical School study, subjects who had high-stress lives but handled them without becoming depressed or anxious were shown to have the highest concentration of natural cancer-killing cells in their bloodstreams than any other group in the study, even more than those who had less stress.

You can't eliminate stress completely. You wouldn't want to. Stress is the creative dynamic that keeps urging us on, despite hardship, to dream and build, to write and create art, to do and be what has never been before. But learning to achieve stress reduction can help you take charge again in a body that may feel very out of control. You can become a partner in the dynamic stress-process, using it for your well-being rather than falling victim to its harmful effects.

In today's world, sometimes you can't fight, you can't flee. The only way out is to learn to flow.
ROBERT ELIOT, M.D.

Take a moment now to try an easy stress-reduction technique. As you inhale, simply say to yourself: *I am* . . . As you exhale, say: . . . *relaxed.* Inhale: *I am* . . . Exhale: . . . *relaxed.* As you close your eyes, let your breathing come naturally, let the words fill the space of your inhalation, the space of your exhalation. Don't force anything. Just let your breathing roll as it will. Continue this process for at least five minutes, and for no more than twenty minutes at a time. You will notice that your breathing slows down and that muscle tension dissipates.

Meditation is another form of relaxation. Dr. Herbert Benson has studied the many biochemical and neurological changes brought about by meditation and recommends a simple exercise he calls the "relaxation response." Benson's approach makes use of a mantra—a centering word or sound—to focus your attention on your breathing to reduce tension and stress. The basic steps of his method are quite simple.

First, assume a comfortable position, although not so comfortable that you are likely to fall asleep. Close your eyes and give yourself a few moments to allow your body to let go. Sink into your chair while still remaining upright, by surrendering your weight but feeling yourself to be supported. Briefly scan your body and try to release tension from head to toe.

Breathing through your nose, internally repeat a simple word or short phrase. Benson recommends the word *one,* but you can use any word that soothes you. Repeat the word with each inhalation, and then again with each exhalation. Focus on your word despite any distracting thoughts, fantasies, and worries that arise. Just allow thoughts to float past you like clouds across a summer sky. If you notice that you are distracted, don't reprimand yourself in any way. Simply go back to the word and resume repeating it.

Continue for about twenty minutes at a time, usually before eating rather than after, as it will slow everything down (including normal digestion). When the twenty minutes have passed, sit quietly and discontinue using the word. Then open your eyes and rest a few minutes more before resuming your normal activities.

Additional stress-reduction techniques can be found in appendix C.

COPING WITH PAIN

Each of you will have to forge a unique path through your own field of pain, aided by your doctor, your medication, your loving friends and care givers, and your own inner guidance. In devoting only a few pages to the subject of pain here, I am not dismissing it lightly. I know it is very important—perhaps paramount—for you.

There is more to pain than the physical sensation. It has tremendous psychological meanings that depend on how the person experiencing it interprets the cause of the pain and its consequences. Fear, above almost everything else, will intensify and maintain pain. Fear causes the body to tense up for protection, and that additional tension may be painful in itself, in addition to aggravating the pain of the original condition.

It is important to break this fear-tension-pain cycle with stress releasers and other forms of relaxation. Breathing exercises, mental imagery, and self-talk have helped many people with pain control. The mind is probably the best pain reliever we can use, and definitely the safest. Other people testify to the analgesic effects of acupuncture, an ancient practice dating back to Stone Age China. For some, massage, pressure point therapy, or the application of heat and cold to the area is effective in reducing or controlling tension and pain.

Since the mid 1970s, when researchers first discovered that the nervous system produces its own morphinelike painkillers, called endorphins, the study of alternative forms of pain control has been intensifying. We are learning more each day about these amazing substances and how they can be released in ways that are within our control—by physical exercise, mental imagery, dietary changes, and even laughter.

The goal of more natural healing approaches is not to eliminate all pain from the human being. Health is not the absence of pain; it is rather the ability to deal effectively with both pleasure and pain. So the suggestions that follow should be read in this light. No one method is offered as a panacea. Most of these alternative methods will require more participation on your part than simply swallowing a pill.

There is nothing wrong with pain medication as prescribed by your doctor. In the acute stages of your health crisis it may be a blessing or a necessity. As you recuperate, however, you would be wise to wean yourself from pain medication as much as possible, so that your body can more effectively work in its own behalf. Anything that promotes expansion in the body and mind allows for more breathing space throughout and diffuses pain, tension, and worry. Here are two exercises designed to assist you in expanding yourself. Several others can be found in appendix D.

A Progressive Expansion

Close your eyes and take a few full, gentle breaths. Begin by focusing attention on your toes and feet, imagining that they are expanding by one inch in every direction.

See this expansion as a cloud of vapor that surrounds each body part. Do it slowly. When you sense that your feet are expanded, move your awareness into your lower legs, then to your knees, your thighs, and gradually up to include your entire body. Feel each area becoming lighter and more buoyant as it expands.

When your whole body is expanded in this way, remain in this state for as long as you wish, but at least for several minutes. Then open your eyes.

Widening the Circle of Pain

If you are in pain, focus on the exact place of greatest intensity. Now take deep breaths, breathing into that place.

In gradual increments expand the pain from the point of focus, allowing it to fill larger and larger spaces in your body. For instance, if your pain is in your lower back, concentrate on the point of origin. Now, in concentric circles, extend it to fill your whole back, your buttocks and thighs, your legs. Move it into your shoulders and upper arms, and so on.

When the pain "fills" your whole body, take it farther still. Have it expand by a foot in every direction around you. Have it fill your bed completely. Fill your room; the house; the whole neighborhood; the town; the state; the country; the planet; the Milky Way galaxy; the entire universe. The wider the pain expands, the more diffused, and thus milder, it becomes.

Continue to expand it infinitely in every direction. Rest.

SUPPORTING THE BODY IN HEALING

Some things are out of our hands. But what we can control we are responsible for. When it comes to supporting the body in the process of healing, there is a lot we can do.

Your body needs rest and good food. It needs to breathe clean air and to breathe more fully. It needs to receive clear light and natural sunlight whenever possible. The body needs to touch and be touched. It needs to move and exercise as appropriate, and it needs to release its tensions and poisons through proper elimination, crying, or other forms of emotional expression; it especially needs to laugh.

Your body is more likely to be healed while in the presence of other healthy people who make it feel good. It needs a minimum of such energy sappers as negative people, and it can't thrive on negative habits like smoking, drinking alcohol, and using drugs. And most of this is in your control.

Let's Consider Food

As Michael recovered from his accident, he spent several weeks in the hospital. His friends cooperated by bringing him freshly squeezed juices and homemade soups as alternatives to the hospital fare. Michael knew that eating highly processed foods—white bread, powdered eggs and potatoes, instant puddings—wasn't really nourishing him in the ways he knew he needed. So he asked for help. Not only were we happy to oblige, we were privileged to have this tangible way to show our caring for him.

As Dick recuperated from his heart attack, he worried a lot about his diet. Knowing that it would mean a big readjustment for his wife and family, he suggested that they attend the nutrition classes offered by the hospital that had treated him. They did. It made the transition into low-fat eating a family affair.

During her recuperation, Harriet found herself craving the soothing foods of her childhood, like tapioca and rice pudding. After consulting with her doctor she arranged for these welcome additions to an otherwise bleak menu.

Scores of conflicting data abound concerning nutritional needs. But in general, you can support and augment the diet suggested by your doctor by remembering that the fresher your food is, the better. The less it is processed, the better. The less salt, fat, sugar, and fewer artificial chemicals it contains, the better.

How you eat is probably as important as *what* you eat. If you eat slowly, savoring your food (even blessing it before you eat), you are more likely to gain the full nutritional benefits; moreover, you will be training yourself to eat less. (Overeating is a common contributor to disease in general.) Eating in a calm atmosphere is invaluable too. That may mean turning off the TV for a while, or asking visitors in the hospital or at home to leave for a short time if it helps you to stay relaxed while eating.

Food is one of your medicines, the raw material you need for your healing. Honor it in this way and you will be taking a strong step forward in the direction of healing and fuller life.

Give Yourself a Rest

Weeks after surgery, many folks find that their energy is still short-lived. If you were always the one with stamina to spare but now find that you're exhausted by lunchtime, that may be hard to take. You may feel embarrassed to admit it, or else guilty that you are being lazy, but in fact you are only experiencing the natural effects of a trauma.

Pushing yourself through the point of exhaustion may be the way to win a marathon, but it is not recommended in the recuperation process. You need to rest, sleep, and relax more than usual, more than you may think is necessary. Healing just takes time.

"Oh sleep! it is a gentle thing, Beloved from pole to pole!" says the ancient Mariner of Coleridge's famous poem. And indeed, sleep is one of the most pleasurable requirements we humans have to fulfill regularly. When we are ill or recuperating, sleep becomes particularly important. It allows the body a chance to mobilize its healing resources: Antibodies build up, bacteria are disposed of, and new cells are produced to replace damaged ones. Sleep is one of the body's strategies for conserving energy and then directing that energy to the places where it is most needed. If we sap these energy reserves repeatedly without replenishing them, we ultimately slow down the process of healing.

While mysteries abound connected with sleep and dreaming, many researchers believe that REM (rapid eye movement) sleep—that stage in which dreaming occurs—is a time for releasing stress. But sleep alone doesn't handle all the physiological and psychological tension that builds up over the course of a day. And to make matters more challenging, many recuperating people find that their sleep patterns are disturbed—by pain, by worry, by the medication they are receiving.

Pain specialist Dr. David Bresler, author of *Free Yourself from Pain*, writes: "Ironically . . . most hypnotic drugs (sleeping pills) significantly suppress REM sleep, causing fewer and shorter REM periods. Consequently, there is a reduced opportunity for stress release." Instead of relying on drugs, Bresler encourages his patients in the practice of relaxation techniques such as those we've reviewed. These exercises promote natural sleep and can be used throughout the day for their stress-releasing effects.

Just because you are not moving around a lot doesn't mean that you are relaxing. Even when the body is still, the mind can be racing out of control, and that may show up as tightened muscles, headaches, intestinal problems, constipation, and so on. That's why, throughout this book, you are advised to learn methods of relaxation that serve to quiet the mind and release unnecessary stress in the body.

Movement and Exercise

Even if you've been told to keep off your feet or if you find yourself in a body cast, you will want to exercise in some way to promote your healing. Mild exercise will keep the energy flowing to the parts that need it the most, will help with pain relief, and will encourage more restful sleep. Drop your unrealistic pictures about training for the Olympics, and allow yourself the adventure of subtle, gentle movement that can be extremely beneficial for you at this time, particularly if you are spending much time in bed.

Exercise does a lot more than simply keep the muscles toned up. It helps you to sleep better, digest your food better, and eliminate more thoroughly. Increased oxygen and blood flow, all results of exercise, help carry necessary nutrients and healing agents to the parts of your body that need them. Remember that old law of physics, Bodies in motion tend to stay in motion, bodies at rest tend to stay at rest?

And exercise is good for the soul, for helping to create a more positive climate for healing. First of all, if you give yourself a couple of short workout sessions every day (even if this means only stretching fingers and toes), you will be breaking up a long day, and this will assist you in relieving the boredom that many recuperating people find so tedious and draining. Second, it will give you small, manageable tasks to accomplish every day, along with ways to chart your progress. "Exercising" some control over yourself and your life in this way will do wonders for your self-esteem. Feeling better about yourself in general, you will be fighting "invalidism," that crippling attitude that fosters separation from life and a sense of helplessness and victimhood. Furthermore, exercise helps in pain control. For example, one of the most annoying problems that can accompany lots of bed rest and chair sitting is that the lower back and other parts get stiff, the buttocks "fall asleep," and the legs get restless. Exercising helps to maintain flexibility and hence mobility. It helps to relieve buildups of pressure and will relax the stiffness.

Here is a simple exercise to try now. Begin by getting quiet. So quiet that you can hear, feel, or at least imagine the beating of your heart, the sound of your lungs as they expand and contract, and the movement of blood flowing up into your brain and all the way down to your feet.

Listen to your breath as it leaves your nostrils or throat. Listen to the sounds of silence inside your head, around your eardrums. Feel yourself swallow. Watch the movement of your diaphragm— up and down, up and down. Become aware of the blinking of your eyes.

Focus your attention on your toes, and then begin to slowly move them in as many ways as you can. Curl them, spread them, tighten them, relax them. Inch by inch and muscle by muscle, begin to move up the body—to the feet, the ankles, the calves, the knees. At each part, direct your full attention there, and then begin to "dance," making tiny, slow movements in as many different ways as are possible and safe for you. (If you have any doubts about this process for yourself, consult your doctor before continuing with any body exercise.) Stop when you reach your waist, and begin again with attention on your fingers. When you finish "dancing" with your shoulders, go back and move from the diaphragm on up to the top of the head.

Take your time with this slow stretch, and enjoy each step of the process. Use music from your radio or tape recorder to enhance the whole experience. As much as possible adopt an attitude of play as you do this. Too many people approach exercise with deadly seriousness. If you're noticing this tendency in yourself, lighten up. A relaxed body is going to move and heal a lot easier. So join the dance.

Appendix E, "Exercise and Play for the Body in Bed," offers useful movements and amusements for almost any condition.

You may be pleasantly surprised to learn that exercise can occur in the mind, even if the body doesn't move. Imagining a series of movements, even without doing them, actually causes muscles to tense and relax in minute degrees, and opens pathways for energy flow. The work of Moshe Feldenkrais, a physicist turned body-educator, was dedicated not to engineering flexible bodies but rather to creating "flexible brains." Feldenkrais taught that setting up a pattern of easeful movement by imaging it first actually prepared the body to move in ways that were gentler and more efficient. Leading the way in application of similar techniques, many athletes from a wide variety of sports are learning that they can practice foul shots, golf swings, ski runs, and overall coordination by visualizing these activities in the mind's eye. The results have been improved performance.

If you have had heart surgery or a heart attack, consult with your doctor about your particular needs. If it is recommended that you participate in a good cardiac rehabilitation program, do it without excuses! (The Reverend Ike used to say, "There is nothing so bad as a good excuse, and the better the excuse, the worse it is.") If you have had orthopedic surgery or an accident of some kind, there is no substitute for your prescribed physical therapy. Inactive muscles lose 15 percent of their strength per week, to be regained only by exercise. A graduated exercise program will normally have your muscles back in shape in six weeks or less.

Les, a young man with serious leg damage following a motorcycle accident, was unmotivated to engage seriously in his exercise

Calorie Burners for Nonathletes

Activity	Calories Burned
Beating around the bush	75
Jogging your memory	125
Jumping to conclusions	100
Climbing the walls	150
Passing the buck	25
Grasping at straws	75
Throwing your weight around	50–300
(depends on your current body weight)	
Dragging your heels	100
Pushing your luck	250
Making mountains out of molehills	500
Spinning your wheels	150
Flying off the handle	225
Running around in circles	350
Chewing nails	200
Eating crow	225
Pouring salt on the wound	25
Hitting bottom	600

See! You have probably been getting more exercise than you thought.

---

program. He had been in the hospital for one month and expected to be there another two. Up until then he exercised only when the physical therapist (PT) moved him. One Saturday when his regular PT was off-duty, a new woman was assigned. He describes their eventful meeting: "She walked into my room and stood at the foot of my bed. 'Why aren't you working out?' she asked challengingly. I protested that it was painful, and besides that I *did* work out three times a week when my regular PT visited me. 'As for today,' I said smugly, 'I've been waiting for you.' A look of incredulity crossed her face. 'Why would you need to wait for me?' she asked. 'You're the only one who's going to get yourself strong again. I can't do that for you. You should be working out all the time.' She was unyielding. Staring me down, she said evenly, 'Well, what else do you have to do with your time?' With that, she turned and left the room. I was shocked at first, enough to take a look at myself, ruthlessly. How thin my body was! How weak! I remember speaking out loud to myself, very slowly, very seriously: 'I'm going to have to pull myself together.' That's when I began. It was none too soon!"

One valuable exercise that is often neglected during recuperation is sex. Especially after heart surgery, recovering patients are fearful that sex may trigger another "accident." Doctors often fail to reassure their patients that most sexual activity requires less effort than moderate walking.

Sex is certainly one of the most highly charged subjects we have to deal with, in or out of bed. If you are concerned about your ability to engage in sex as a result of your accident or injury, or if you are troubled by the fear of being unattractive or unacceptable as a sex partner, please speak to your doctor or primary care givers. As delicate as this subject is, it is essential that you share your fears if they are to be dealt with. And the good news is that there is help available to you from many sources. Many counselors and therapists deal specifically with sexuality issues of the sick and handicapped. There are others to talk to who have faced and successfully overcome the same problems that may seem insurmountable for you.

Sexual energy is life energy. It stirs things up, inside and out, and gets you moving, which is exactly what your body needs right now. It may be necessary to modify your lovemaking to suit your body's current condition, but the closeness and caring that accompany sex will be another of your very best medicines. Shere Hite, the famed poll taker in the field, says that "sex is intimate physical contact for pleasure. There is never any reason to think that the 'goal' must be intercourse." You too may discover a whole new approach to sex that is less pressured, gentler, and ultimately more satisfying.

Please Touch

Experts tell us that humans and other mammals experience an actual skin hunger, a need for touch that must be satisfied in developing human infants. When you are sick in bed, recuperating, you may experience this skin hunger as a nagging sense of loneliness, irritability, or powerful appetite for food. You may not realize that what you are really hungry for is a hand to hold.

Bear in mind, however, that friends and family may treat you as if you were infectious. They may hold back in touching you because they are afraid—of catching something; of hurting you ("Sick people are delicate and may break if squeezed too hard"); of confronting their own fears of illness. A gift you can give your visitors is the assurance that you recognize their fears. A greater gift is your invitation that they deal with their fears directly and start touching you, if that is what you want.

If you happen to be in the hospital, you've probably already noticed that there are unwritten taboos against physical intimacy. I always offer my recuperating friends the opportunity for a foot massage when I visit them. But when I've done this, on various occasions, it has been in spite of discouraging looks from the hospital staff.

Glenda, one of my former students and an oncology nurse in a busy suburban hospital, learned a dramatic lesson about the value of touch from one of her patients, thirty-four-year-old Ronnie, suffering with terminal cancer. As Glenda left Ronnie's room one evening, having taken her temperature and pulse and administered medication, Ronnie called out to her. "Even you, Glenda? Is everybody around here going to treat me like a statistic?"

Glenda described the scene with heartfelt words: "I lost all my professional composure in that moment. All the protective layers I had constructed for myself suddenly dissolved. We were no longer nurse and patient; I was now simply a woman standing in a room with a sister or friend—one who hurt, who was lonely. And her pain and loneliness were mine. Her question became a challenge to me, and I knew that I had a critical decision to make. If I turned away now or gave her a cursory, 'professional' response, I would be choosing a direction for the rest of my career. I would be an efficient nurse, but that prize would come at the expense of my soul.

"So I chose to hear her. Without hesitation I closed the door to her room, removed my shoes and cap, put down my clipboard full of charts, carefully maneuvered around the tubes that connected her to a food supply, and climbed into the bed with her. We both started to cry. Then we fell asleep. My supervisors never mentioned the incident. For me it was transforming. I'm not the same nurse I was before meeting Ronnie. I think I'm a better one."

There is real healing that happens in the close physical proximity of another human body. The "laying on of hands" that faith healers use today is the last remnant of age-old practices in which the shaman used his or her entire body to free the afflicted person from an evil spirit. In Reiki, a form of Japanese energy-balancing work, for example, the therapist helps the client release stored muscular tension and pain in parts of the body by simply placing hands on the area in question and leaving them there for five to fifteen minutes at a time.

Dorothy, at age sixty-eight, survived a head-on car collision. At the hospital, in excruciating pain, she knew from previous experience that physical touch and massage would help her more than any other remedies. "I told my doctor that I needed it," she related with conviction. "I knew that if I simply *asked* for it, he would say no. So I told him!" And he listened. He even wrote her a prescription for massage as part of her physical therapy. "All I looked forward to during those long days was that massage. It relieved my pain, and it helped ease the tension that was building up in me due to so much lying around."

You do have access to the healing physical presence of others, and you are probably going to have to ask for it. *You* are going to have to initiate it, as Dorothy did, to get your needs met. You may need no convincing of how wonderful it is to be touched and massaged, especially if you are confined to bed. What you may need is encouragement to ask for this touching. Well, here's the permission and the motivation: *It's good for you!*

Massage will relieve tension, and thus help to alleviate pain and stiffness in your body. It stimulates blood flow and electrical energy in your nervous system to wake up the parts of you that are going to sleep. It will also help in breaking up the emotional blockages caused by your trauma. And best of all, it just feels good.

You don't need a professional to get the nurturing and healing benefits of massage. If you are lucky enough to have a friend or care giver willing to give you a massage—a back or foot rub, a scalp massage, a facial, or more—speak up. Tell your friend what feels good, where to work harder or softer. Trust that what feels good is just what you need. Keep in mind that you are doing your visitors a favor by your specific request. Give them this book and invite them to read the letter that follows:

An Open Letter to a Touching Friend

You are about to offer the highest service possible to your recuperating friend or patient. Your touch can be their healing.

Relax. You don't need any prior experience to make this an exquisite gift. As you touch, you will be communicating your love and caring through your hands. With that as your motivation you will be better, in some ways, than a professional.

Touching, in massage, establishes a connection of the heart between the partners involved, so approach your task with respect. The more you can let go of the chatter and judgment in your mind about whether or not you're doing it "right" and allow your hands to move intuitively, the more relaxed and wonderful the results will be.

Do the massage as a gift to yourself as well. Put on some music and allow your hands to dance as they make contact with your friend's body. Keep making movements that feel smooth and flowing to you.

Use all parts of your hands: palms, fingers, fingertips, knuckles, backs. Use your wrists, your forearms, your elbows.

Vary your strokes in many ways. Pat gently, roll the skin between your fingers, knead, slap, tap with fingertips. Create a rhythm. Establish a pattern, and then break it and try a new one. Keep amusing and nurturing yourself. Imagine that your friend is really yourself, and give him or her all the love and caring that you want the world to give you.

Use a light lotion, not oil (it may stain sheets), if your friend wants it. Warm the lotion in your hands before applying it to the skin.

Keep your movements flowing, continuous. Begin softly, and end slowly and softly as well. Conclude by simply leaving your hands in contact with your friend's body for a minute or more, and then remove them gently.

Thank you for this gift of yourself.

Sometimes a genuine hug is all you need to make your day. Yet many folks don't give themselves permission to hug or hold in a way that really allows for a merging of life-energy. The hug that is healing is the hug that allows you to relax into another's arms, if only for a few seconds, to feel the tangible, physical support of another human being. You might suggest that your friend or care giver give you a "breakfast hug," my term for a gentle but complete embrace in which one partner acts as the warm toast, the other partner as the butter. Maintain the contact until both of you agree that the butter is completely melted, absorbed into the toast.

If you don't have a friendly hugger or massage therapist around, you don't necessarily need to go hungry. There are ways to massage yourself—foot reflexology, for instance—that help to relieve pain, balance energy, and satisfy a longing for nurturance. See appendix E for suggestions.

Fresh Air and Sunlight

Take a look around your room—the room in which you spend most of your time during the course of any particular day. Take a whiff of the air, while you're at it! Ask yourself one very important question: Does this room support living and growing things?

A good clue to the answer is whether or not a green plant could thrive there. Is there enough natural light and sunlight for that? Is there adequate moisture in the air? Does the air circulate frequently, or does it feel (and smell) stale? How can you expect to thrive if a plant would have to struggle?

Your body needs light to maintain its balance. When light enters the eyes, it passes along neurochemical channels to the pineal and pituitary glands. These are the master controllers of the endocrine system. Any change in endocrine balance will cause corresponding alterations in body chemistry and even in physiology. Light has been shown to be a contributing factor in the amount of milk a cow produces, the number of eggs a chicken lays, and the physical development of children.

The pioneering work of John Ott and other researchers suggests that natural light is highly preferable to artificial light and especially to fluorescent lighting, which often lacks the near-ultraviolet portion of the light spectrum. He suggests, as I do, that you make use of natural light whenever possible. If you are well enough to move to a sunny spot in the house for at least a short time each day, do it. If you can get outside for a little while, so much the better. Use sunscreen lotions for any more than brief exposure, but don't let that discourage you from taking advantage of nature's healing source—the power of the sun. Appendix F suggests other ways to make your recuperation room a place that supports life and growth.

Looking Better and Feeling Better

In the beginning stages of an illness or in the shock phase of an accident, you will have all you can do just to meet your survival needs for sleep, nourishment, and pain control. When that phase is over and you itch to start moving again, begin a short daily routine of self-care for looking and feeling better. Among other things, it provides another way to structure some of the endless time you have on your hands.

There is a fine line to be walked as you attend to your physical appearance in bed or around the house as you recuperate. You certainly do not need to burden yourself with looking "good as new." In fact, if you try, you will probably be pushing too hard. On the other hand, there is a definite energy attached to cleanliness, to order, and especially to bright, warm color. What you see when you look in the mirror is going to affect the way you feel.

Here are a few ways to enhance your body image, to lift your spirits, and to make good use of your time as you recuperate:

- Get a haircut, change the style. Even asking a friend to simply wash your hair for you and then dry it and brush it will provide a welcome change.
- Get a manicure or a pedicure. This doesn't need to be done by a professional either; any caring friends will do. And while they're at it, ask them to massage your hands and feet. That will simulate a massage to the whole body.
- Attend to your teeth and gums. Give yourself a gum massage. (A finger will do this job nicely.) Keep a toothbrush, floss, and toothpicks near your bed and use them often. Rinse your mouth frequently with a natural mouthwash, one or two drops of oil of peppermint in a quart of water.
- Wear warm, lively, or tranquil colors to suit your moods. Many people find that bright primary colors have an arousing and stimulating effect on them. Pastels and blues seem to induce a more tranquilizing effect. Choose colors that bring out a healthy glow in your skin tone and experience how that elevates your spirits.
- Dress for energy. Take off those crumpled old pajamas if you are tired of them. No law says that you must wear pajamas in the hospital or in the house during your recuperation. Why not jogging pants and bright shirts? Many women enjoy beau-

tiful nightgowns and bed gowns or soft jackets. Suit yourself, but consider color, texture, and whatever else about your clothing that makes you feel more alive.

- Do facial exercises to soften lines and tone muscles. You can make these up for yourself or experiment with some regular ones—the Lion from hatha-yoga, for example. Take a deep breath and then hold it as you open your mouth and stick out your tongue, pointing it as far as you can toward your chin. At the same time, stretch your eyes open as wide as they will go. Hold this pose for a count of five, and then exhale and release it. Do it three times at each session.

  Or try giving yourself a facial massage. Knead, slap, stroke, and roll the skin on your face (gently around your eyes). Consider that you are trying to wake up all the cells and increase circulation throughout your face.

- Treat your skin to a moisturing lotion or cream, or even an oil treatment. (Natural almond oil, sesame oil, or olive oil is wonderful for this, but be prepared to change the sheets; oils will stain.) Give special care to the parts of your body that are often neglected—your lower legs and ankles and feet, your upper arms and elbows, your buttocks and lower back.

- Try something out for fun. Try repainting your cast, putting on a hat or bright-colored scarf, adding a temporary tattoo to a place where only your doctor will find it. One man I know donned a gorilla mask whenever sober visitors were expected. In short, have a good time, and show it.

TRUSTING THE BODY— LISTENING TO YOURSELF

Now that you are laid up, you are likely to hear everyone's recuperation stories: "When I broke my leg the itching inside the cast was enough to drive me crazy. . . ." "I'd never want to go through *that* again." "The best thing to do for . . ." You will get advice and prescriptions and maybe even a few horror stories, so just be prepared.

Remember first of all that this is *your body, your home.* Nobody else feels exactly what you feel. You are unique. Attunement to your own body and self-trust are your strongest assets in healing. You know a great deal more about your body and what works for you than you may be willing to admit. So listen to yourself. Follow your own cues. You now have the luxury of quiet time in which to do some of this fine-tuning.

Trusting yourself means following your own rhythm. This can mean eating when you are hungry, sleeping when you feel tired, working during times of the day that are the most productive for you. Your body has experienced a shock that has upset your well-worn patterns and responses. Here is an unequalled opportunity for you to break with old programs—those dictated by the clock or social convenience—in favor of a lifestyle of increased self-attunement, spontaneity, and trust.

Trusting yourself means "listening" for the internal feedback that your food, drugs, or therapy are offering. If you continually feel deenergized or more anxious after eating certain foods, that may indicate a necessary diet change. Question your doctor about the side effects of the drugs you are taking, and inquire about alternatives to drug treatment. Learn by observing yourself the difference between helpful pain and harmful pain as you undertake your physical therapy. If you feel that something is "not right" about a suggested method or treatment, trust yourself enough to honor this intuition. Ask, and be persistent in your request for an answer that you can really understand.

Trusting yourself may mean saying, "no, thank you," when necessary. You can say no to prospective visitors, to demands on your time or energy, to the doctor who does not listen to you in favor of one who does. Trusting yourself means telling yourself the whole truth—about what you can and can't do, what you do and don't want. If you try to trick yourself into doing something before the time is right, your body will retaliate for its own protection. Learn your own tendencies. Don't start to rock 'n' roll while the rhythm in your body is still a waltz. On the other hand, don't stay a wallflower when you've heard and felt the invitation to join the dance of life again.

HONOR THE CONNECTION OF BODY, MIND, AND SOUL

For a long time the pejorative term *psychosomatic* was the only one around that reflected the connection between the body (soma) and the mind (psyche) in health and illness. To most of the general public, this came to mean "the pain is only in your head." But some understood its real meaning, that what goes on in our minds will show up in the body. The fact that more and more of us accept without question that worry contributes to the formation of ulcers, that fear can trigger asthmatic attacks, is actually a major shift in the thinking of the culture. The long-standing mind/body dualism upon which many of our institutions have been built is being seriously reexamined. Cracks in this once secure foundation are widening daily as we become more sophisticated medical consumers. A visit to a bookstore today will reveal a whole new vocabulary in medicine and self-care. Doctors currently explore such fields as psychoneuroimmunology and psychobiology. Words like *wellness* and *bodymind* (which links the parts together into a dynamic whole) are appearing with greater regularity in the popular media.

My body is like the earth, whose mountains, valleys, riverbed, and uneven topography tell the story of its history and creation as surely as my body expresses the trials and creative changes that I have experienced throughout my lifetimes.

KEN DYCHTWALD, *Bodymind*

The pioneering work of Wilhelm Reich, Ida Rolf, and their successors in the research of body structure and emotional states suggests that the body, like the mind, is a huge memory bank, storing all kinds of memories, feelings, pains. For example, if as a child you fell off your bike and landed on your back, that area may hold not only the scars but the sense of panic and abandonment you may have felt at the time. Years later, sometimes without warning, another trauma or even a touch to this area can loosen up this old business again. It is as if you have a "mind" that includes a memory in every cell. The body and the emotions are connected in ways that we are understanding more and more.

Susan, a professional massage therapist, has many recuperating people among her clients. As she works with them, applying her hands to certain pressure points in the body, emotions and memories may be released. Often someone will burst into tears and be surprised by the intensity of the response. Another will recall a dramatic moment from childhood that he hadn't thought of in years just because Susan is holding or moving his arm or leg in a certain way. "It reminds me of the way a bird flies from a box when the lid is lifted," she says. "Sometimes it is a bird of sadness, sometimes of anger, and sometimes one of joy."

Imagine the emotional repercussions of open-heart surgery. Just think of how much "stuff" has been collected around the heart, both physically and emotionally—every close brush with death, every lost love. . . . And now that part of the body is being cut open, the heart itself exposed. And while this may constitute a miracle for some, it is also a major intervention in the body that is bound to stir up some very strong emotions. When this happens we are suddenly more vulnerable in ways that we may have avoided for years, even a lifetime. Depression is one result. Even though we are healing, even though life may be extended, we feel sad.

In *A Change of Heart,* author Nancy Yanes Hoffman interviews people who have had open-heart surgery. One man reveals: "I'm depressed because my body was violated and opened up, because my chest was cracked open; I'm depressed because I was like a frog on the table. . . . That's me, the frog prince, only more frog than prince. I feel terribly violated. Still."

As you recuperate, you will have ample opportunity to experience for yourself this connection of body, mind, and soul—ways that may be fascinating, ways that may be very painful. Keep in mind that there is no place that the body starts and the mind and soul stop, and vice versa. Honoring the body in bed means honoring every aspect of yourself.

STEP 3

Keep Time with Yourself

Sitting silently.
Doing nothing.
Spring comes.
And the grass grows by itself.
BASHO (JAPANESE POET)

When we are sick or hurting, we want to get it over with, fast, so we can get right back to a normal life again. We especially hate the sense of wasting time. But the fact is, things almost always take longer than we expect, be it cleaning out the garage, waiting for a friend who promises to be "just five more minutes," or regaining our strength after a major illness.

It's no wonder we are impatient. We are affected by what psychiatrist Theodore Isaac Rubin calls time pollution—the "din of time" that is always there in our mind, demanding that we perform and produce. It seems more and more to be an assumption among people I know that faster is better. Rubin notes: "As stimulation addicts, we jump from point to point as the culture changes at fantastic speed and makes demands on us to change accordingly." This "future shock" has indeed become our present reality. But it is one for which we are paying dearly in other, more stressful ways.

RESPECT CONVALESCENCE

You may feel anxious as you find yourself facing a period of slow-down because our culture's messages about "faster is better" are deeply ingrained in you, too. As Don healed slowly from his heart

50

condition, he was shocked at how many of his friends and colleagues expected him to be back at work soon again. "They were
only too quick to suspect that I was taking advantage of my time
off."

What has happened to the idea of convalescence as a time for
rest and renewal? One hardly even hears that word anymore. Convalescence conjures up pictures or stories of another place and
time, of people retiring to the seaside or traveling to the spas or
mineral baths of Europe for fresh air, clean water, long slow walks
in the countryside. Few recuperating people interviewed for this
book did anything *like* that during this time.

Ours is a culture that prizes effort, hard work, and results.
"Just dig in and get the job done as quickly as possible." "Stay up
all night if you have to, but meet the deadline." And while this
might work with a business project or preparations for your daughter's wedding, it is ultimately unsuitable as a tactic for recuperation. Your body is not a project or a party. Neither is it a machine.

You cannot force yourself to get well, except temporarily;
eventually the body will have its way. One of the most effective
ways to sabotage your recuperation is to try to rush the process,
especially in the early stages. Bodies, minds, and spirits take time
to heal—lots of time.

What will it take to transform recuperation into something
more like convalescence? Is it possible to approach your healing
process as a chance for rest and renewal—an opportunity, albeit
an enforced one, to relax the usual pressures for immediate results? Can you stretch your imagination far enough to think of this
time as a "vacation" of self-discovery in which you take a long,
slow, gentle "walk" within? I believe it is entirely feasible to rein-
terpret the notion of "taking advantage of time off" to mean something positive and life-supporting.

In Your Own Good Time

My dear friend Anita was out of the hospital after major surgery
when she called for help. She was discouraged. She needed support.

For three days I cooked for her and cleaned the house and
rubbed her feet, listened to her, and held her when she cried. It

was a healing time for both of us. I soon learned that Anita was playing a game with herself, a self-destructive game of comparison with others. She told me that a woman she knew who had had the same operation was back to work within four days. She told me about another woman whose scars were practically invisible after a week. She looked at herself, knowing that she'd never beat this record, and felt depressed.

Anita is one of the brightest, most independent women I know, a real mover in life. But like so many of us, she had been bitten by the bugs of impatience and comparison, and she was feeling the effects all over.

So we talked about time, about how healing can take a lot of it. We concentrated on her own special time schedule and the wastefulness of comparison with others. Listen, I told her, you're going to hear a lot of exaggerations and downright lies from some of the most well-meaning people. They tell you how fast it's going to be over. How speedy recovery was for them. But the truth is, most of us have very selective memories. We sometimes glorify the past in our misguided attempt to make somebody feel better. And in reality, we may end up creating more misery when someone can't measure up to our standards. On the other hand, some people maybe *have* healed more quickly than you. They may have had a different energy level, a different attitude, a different chemistry— who knows? You can make yourself extremely unhappy trying to figure it out. So stop it. Honor your body now. Love it now. Give it as much positive attention as you can . . . now.

Some people need more sleep than others. Some of us are night people, others are early-morning people. The same variations of need and preference show up in food choice, in exercise programs, in the type of work we do. The point is, why should it not also be present in our healing rhythms as well? Sure, there are average recovery periods, but don't forget that to get to an average you add up the high scores and the very low scores and arrive someplace in the middle. In my own case, following hepatitis, it was a full year before I could honestly report feeling like my old self again. For my friend Kathy it took more than twice as long.

Trust the time it takes for you to heal without comparing yourself with others. This will serve you in everything you undertake for the rest of your life.

The Thousand Things

It also takes time to adjust to the thousands of changes that your recovery requires, whether the changes are tiny or monumental.

A stroke patient will often have to relearn how to speak. A heart patient will usually have to radically change his or her diet and working habits. The survivor of a serious accident who has lost the use of an arm or leg, even temporarily, will have to learn a full range of adaptive behaviors. And that is just the physical end of the process.

Emotional adjustment may take a lot longer. How infuriating it may be to have to call your wife or child every time you want to get a box from the top shelf of your closet, how humiliating to require assistance in taking a bath! The thousand things that normal people do routinely and take for granted may, for you, require intense effort and hours more time.

Remember that compassion for yourself will be your greatest asset. Take it easy. I know that discouragement grows when, day after day, you don't see or feel much improvement. The fact is that sometimes things get worse just before they get better. Also, because we are anticipating a big change too fast we often miss the subtle indications of returning strength. We easily forget that healing is not a straight-line function. Drawn on a graph, your improvement over time would look more like a jagged edge or a series of ocean waves, with numerous peaks and valleys reflecting your up days and down days. Nevertheless, the line would be projecting forward and upward. But in order to see the overall pattern, you'd have to stand back from it. Right in the middle of a crisis, one point on the line, it is hard to be aware of movement or change. The big picture is appreciated only over time.

Brenda, a nurse who for ten years has been the director of cardiac rehabilitation at a major hospital, stresses that recovery is a slow process. As she tells her patients, "You didn't create your heart condition in a single day—and you won't remedy it overnight either." Her advice is fundamental, and one of the basic principles of the fine art of recuperation. Allow yourself the luxury of time for complete and gentle healing. Like a seed that first must die before it can sprout, or a caterpillar in its dark and lonely cocoon, things sometimes appear to be their worst just before they start to get better.

MAKING A FRIEND OF TIME

Only 1,440—that's all we have. One thousand, four hundred forty minutes in one day. Whether you are president of the corporation or a worker on the line, you get the same number. It is one of the few things in life distributed equally.

Experts in the field of time management tell us that the perception of time—whether it seems to be moving fast or slow, whether we seem to have enough or too much—depends largely on how we regard it. Is time a friend, something that supports and challenges us, or an enemy, something we must be armed against?

Dick, the owner of a successful heating business, suffered a heart attack and underwent surgery at age fifty-one. As he related to me, "I was into making money, lots of money. I always told myself that 'after this job' I'd take a vacation, but I never did. My typical day started at 4:00 A.M. and ended about 10:00 P.M. when I collapsed exhausted into bed. I had to personally supervise every single job! The night before my surgery I was on the phone to subcontractors and employees, until the nurses noticed that my blood pressure was reaching a danger point."

When I asked Dick how the business was going now, three months after his operation, he admitted that he was not anxious to get back to work. "I learned that I wasn't as indispensable as I thought I was," he admitted. "My brother is running the business now almost as well as I did. At first I thought I couldn't take this staying home, resting, going for walks. But now I've really come to enjoy it."

Dick had made a friend of time. His story affirms that people can adjust to change and come to treasure it, even though they may start out resisting it all the way.

What is your relationship with time? Chances are, like most of us, it is sometimes good, sometimes not so good. "When I am feeling okay about me, I am synchronized with life in general," wrote Sarah, a woman who has an advanced degree in this fine art of recuperation due to her many bouts with illness. "When I'm feeling up, time poses no problems. I may have to speed up to make an appointment or slow down to really hear what is being said to me, but either way I still remain on time—which for me means in balance, content. The opposite is also true. When I am down on myself, feeling discouraged, unloved and unlovable, I don't flow with anything, including time. Deadlines are missed. I sleep longer but don't feel rested. Boredom prevails."

It seems as if making a friend of time has a lot to do with making friends with yourself. Following are some practical considerations to help you do both.

Live One Day at a Time

There is no better way to heal an illness, withstand pain, or fully experience pleasure than to live it moment to moment, one day at a time.

Trying to anticipate how you are ever going to get through "three months of this" is not only frightening or frustrating but most likely a waste of valuable energy. (And besides, it doesn't leave any room for the possibility of miracles, which always happen when we least expect them!)

Marge, a sixty-eight-year-old woman who spent seven months in a full-body cast, put it this way:

> I would start worrying about how I could ever live through another five or six months in my plaster prison. Then it occurred to me that if I just postponed my worrying until tomorrow morning, I would be better able to deal with it. For today, I would simply take it easy. When tomorrow was today, I would once again put off my worrying until tomorrow. The great thing about doing this is that tomorrow never came. So all I ever had to manage was *today.*

Now, some would argue that, like Scarlett O'Hara, Marge had adopted an "I'll think about it tomorrow" strategy that could give way to irresponsibility, to avoiding facing up to real and logical consequences. And indeed, this could be so. But not in Marge's case. She had discovered that by confining her suffering within day-tight compartments, she could handle it. Otherwise, the pain could easily have overwhelmed her.

You too can deal with today. Even if this moment is the worst yet, you are surviving it. And remember, there is almost always help available today, even right now, if you are willing to ask for it. Why postpone relief? Start playing as if today is all there is, and do whatever it takes to make this the best possible day. Why wait to call that friend? Why wait to start that exercise program? Why worry another day when a phone call to your doctor would answer that troublesome question?

---

*Truth has no special time of its own.
Its hour is now . . . always.*
ALBERT SCHWEITZER

Start Living Now, and Right Where You Are

Attention please, ladies and gentlemen in bed, recuperating: This period is not time off from your life. This *is* your life, right now.

It is a funny thing, but I have noticed that most human beings act as if they were rehearsing for the day when their "real lives" finally start. As a child, I spent September and October anticipating Thanksgiving vacation, and thereafter expecting Christmas. After the first of the year, there was nothing to look forward to until Easter, and then summer vacation, and then . . . And embarrassed as I am to admit it, I still operate this way a great deal of the time.

Waiting, stalling until the stage is finally complete so that we can begin the show, fantasizing how happy and fulfilled we will be when our ship comes in at last, we miss. As my husband's eighty-five-year-old aunt loved to joke: "I looked so long at the neighboring green pastures that when I finally got up the courage to make a move I was too old to jump the fence!"

There is life oozing up everywhere at this very moment, right under your nose. Admittedly, it takes a lot of dedication to live in this present reality. I know. I "check out" on myself hundreds of times a day. Eating my carefully prepared breakfast cereal, full of fresh strawberries and bananas, I'm planning what to make for supper. By the time my bowl is empty, I'm looking for another because I never really tasted the first.

But what if the present moment is full of anguish and pain? Isn't it helpful to distract ourselves from it? Well, yes and no. If every time a wave of fear arises you automatically take a drug or turn on the TV, you may never get to move through the fear to discover the strength that awaits on the other side. On the other hand, just letting your fears run rampant, letting your mind play them over and over again, is decidedly unhelpful. Disciplined or conscious use of distraction (such as focusing on breathing, or laughing, or singing with awareness) can be extremely valuable. An old Chinese proverb reminds us that we may not be able to stop the birds from flying around our heads, but we can definitely prevent them from building their nests in our hair.

Understand, this is not a simple task, this learning to stay conscious to all the flavors of life. It is the work of a lifetime, actually. So please don't be easily discouraged.

Living right now does not exclude making decisions or plans. In this moment, your joy may be to organize a party for your daughter's next birthday, to read up on political issues so that you can be a more informed voter, or to talk with friends or associates about next week's business deal. *You can still live in the moment and plan for the future.* Simply enjoy your *planning* fully, while dropping expectations of exactly how the future will or should turn out.

Life is a process to be lived, not a project to be completed. Your recuperation is a process. Remember that. Live it!

Drop Untimely Thinking: "If Only . . ." "I'll Never . . ." and So On

Illnesses and accidents rarely come at the right time. You might be telling yourself that you would have been better able to handle your crisis if it had come next week, or after this project was completed, or during the winter so that you wouldn't miss your vacation. And you might be right. But what good will it do you to bother yourself in this way now? It is useless to fight what is and will only result in you creating additional stress for yourself.

Another way we sabotage our healing time is by berating ourselves: "If only I hadn't done this . . ." or "If only I had done that . . . but now it's too late." The "if only" mind-game is only one of many types of untimely thinking that may plague you in your unguarded moments as you live out your recuperation. Perhaps you will catch yourself in all-or-nothing thinking—"My doctor didn't call today; I'm firing her!" Or maybe catastrophic thinking—"Nothing is ever going to change and will probably only get worse."

What would you say to a best friend with this kind of untimely thinking on the brain? You'd probably fire off a "Quit it, because it simply isn't true!" So be your own best friend right now. Talk to yourself! Or call a friend whose opinion you trust, and do some reality testing: "Hey, Fred, I've been thinking like this . . . Does that sound realistic to you, or what?"

Sometimes repeating a phrase that turns the thinking around might also prove helpful. These self-designed statements, such as "Time is on my side and I am on my side, and I am healing more each day," are called affirmations. They help break untimely thinking patterns and give you a time-out in which to catch your breath. We'll have more to say about affirmations in step 7.

Transforming untimely thinking into positive action is one powerful way of making a friend of time. The presence of these thought patterns may provide the perfect opportunity in which to substitute relaxation. Instead of berating what is or blaming yourself, instead of ruining your precious time by imagining the worst, why not try breathing "in time," in a way that actually reduces your stress? In my own experience, relaxed breathing seems to calm my worrying mind and strengthen me in my ability to cope with the things that are bothering me. You may want to refer again to appendix C for breathing exercises. Or try this approach to balancing out: Inhale slowly, counting 1,000 . . . 2,000 . . . 3,000 . . . 4,000 . . . , imagining that you are pulling the air in through your feet and up to the top of your head. Hold the breath for a few seconds and then exhale to the same count—1,000 . . . 2,000 . . . 3,000 . . . 4,000 . . .—releasing the air down the back of your body and out your feet. Close your eyes and try it for five or ten minutes at a time.

TIME ON YOUR HANDS: WHAT TO DO

John, a forty-seven-year-old businessman, refers to himself as an entrepreneur. Eight years ago, after many years as a long-distance semi-truck driver, he had back surgery to correct a genetic disk problem. A long recovery period left him anxious and bored until he came up with a plan. "I knew I needed a goal," John remarked, "something to concentrate on to help me pass the hours away. TV just wasn't enough. So I made a list of all the books I ever wanted to read, and every week my wife would get some from the library and I would devour them. By the time I got through them all, I was well and ready to go back to work. I didn't work as a trucker much longer, though. Within the year I had started my own business, and I'm proud to say I'm fairly successful at it."

Like John, you may experience the anxiousness and boredom that come with long hours and little to do. Impatience grows as energy builds but finds no constructive outlet, yet this impatience may be a milestone in your healing process. It means that you have energy to spare (even if it is purely mental). This is the energy that you will want to channel in a healthy way. Ignoring your impatience will often encourage unhealthy expression: overeating, smoking, drug or alcohol use, blaming others. Choosing how to channel your energy really means deciding how you will spend your time.

Most people find that in the early days of recuperation they want only light, "mindless" activities or diversions to help pass the time. After that, some will choose to build their "channel" deeper, to cultivate longtime interests there has been no opportunity to pursue, to further explore current hobbies or subjects of study. Others will build their "channels" wider, by expanding into brand-new territory. Perhaps you'll do both. If you are ready to stretch your creative muscles, there are limitless possibilities available right now, no matter what your physical restrictions may be.

You've probably dreamed, at some point in your life, of having uninterrupted time to start new projects, to finish old ones, to think, to plan, to read, to pray, to just fool around. The remainder of this step will offer you the chance to recall some of these dreams. Simply remembering and listing them can be entertainment in itself. Remember, the more ideas you generate, the more possibilities you have to choose from. This was precisely the process that resulted for me in the idea for this book. Who knows what *you'll* discover?

As you start generating ideas of things to do with your time (even if the list is only in your head), keep a few things in mind:

- Don't censor your ideas, especially for feasibility or financial practicality. Sometimes a totally impossible item will lead you quite naturally to one that is easy to implement. In other words, don't limit yourself. Think big!
- Keep a sense of lightness, even humor if possible, as you

recall your interests and options. Don't take your fun too seriously. It really is okay to enjoy yourself.

- Relieve yourself of the burden of having to finish everything you start. If a book you're reading doesn't uplift you, put it away and read another. The same holds true for projects. *Have fun.*

It's all right to have a good time. That's one of the most important messages of enlightenment.

THADDEUS GOLAS,
The Lazy Man's Guide to Enlightenment

Do Something to Enrich Your Time

Maybe you've always wanted to write poetry. Or perhaps you'd like to paint a picture—of anything. I know a man who makes a habit of learning something new every day, even if it's only one fact he has gleaned from the encyclopedia. Learning is an important key to using time when you are ill. There is so much to enjoy in this world. Yet when we are healthy we are so busy going about day-to-day survival we often allow ourselves little free time in which to feed our souls.

Illness can be a mountaintop experience, providing us with a new perspective from which to see and appreciate things. I have found that being in bed, limited in my ability to travel or even to move around, has usually inspired in me an increased desire to see the world, to understand history, to appreciate art. How about you? What would you like to know about? All right, so you cannot go to Beijing today, but maybe you've always been fascinated by Chinese culture or art, or perhaps you'd like to speak the language. Once you focus on what it is that you've always wanted to try, you will find a wealth of information available through books, tapes, movies, and even in conversations with your visitors.

Years ago, during an extended recuperation period, I took up the study of parapsychology, a field that had interested me but in which I had no background or experience. I practiced experiments in extrasensory perception (ESP) and psychokinesis (PK), trying to move bits of tissue paper on my bed table using only the power of my mind. (It didn't work.) Fascinated, I read about the occult roots and the scientific research and the modern theories, about what was being explored in Russia at the time. Soon psychic healing became a consuming interest, and I branched into the study of reincarnation and "after-death" phenomena. I actually turned myself into an expert. Six months after my surgery I taught a course in parapsychology at the local community college. Eight years later I was still a respected member of the part-time faculty. My diversion had opened a new world for me, and it became the foundation for my future work in wellness and holistic health and started me into the study of death and dying, grief and loss, which is what I teach today.

Art, architecture, music, medicine, history, psychology, sports, mythology, literature, science, religion—start jogging your memory by thinking of major departments a university might have. Then go on to explore "minors" within that field. For instance, if your interest is art, is your focus art history, the paintings of van Gogh, graffiti, or sculpture in ancient Greece? Narrowing down your topic may help give some structure to your investigation and prevent you from feeling overwhelmed as you begin. On the other hand, you might just want to read or study randomly in the field, just for the fun of it.

Are there games you've always wanted to learn but have never taken the time? Bridge, Chess, Go? What an ideal opportunity to acquaint yourself with a person who might teach you the game—and who would also provide you with an interesting and regular visitor.

Who are your heros or heroines? People you have heard about, even been inspired by, but about whom you know very little. Biographies or autobiographies of other human beings can be valuable as you recuperate. Everybody has had obstacles to meet, pain to endure. Some will have stories to tell that will speak directly to what you are experiencing right now. Some will assist you by making you laugh, others by letting you cry.

Where would you like to travel? Travel is one of the surest ways of expanding your knowledge and appreciation of yourself and others. And the next-best thing to traveling with your body is traveling with your heart and your imagination. Don't limit yourself to places along the beaten track. Perhaps you want to travel to Antarctica or deep into the forests of Borneo. There's nothing like a few issues of *National Geographic* to remind you of the wonders of the world.

If you are having difficulty thinking of what interests you might have, check appendix G for a list of "memory joggers" and an exercise to help you select topics to explore.

Do Something to Pass the Time

Simple, repetitious activities like knitting, rug hooking, or crossword puzzles are popular with recuperating people. They help pass the time and can be done almost anywhere—sitting in bed, waiting in the doctor's office, while watching TV. These manageable tasks show immediate results, something that may be lacking in other aspects of your life.

Have you ever considered the option of coloring or painting? A set of colored pencils (my favorite), markers, crayons, or easy-to-apply paints and a coloring book or paint-by-numbers kit can provide hours of interest. Coloring books today are not merely the cartoon compendiums they used to be—they can actually teach you things like anatomy or biology or how to identify wildflowers. Check the Drawing and Coloring section in appendix G; you may find yourself inspired to create something of your own design.

Do Something to Escape Time

We've put a lot of emphasis on the active part of time management as you recuperate. There is another, more passive side, however, in which you can allow yourself to *be* entertained, to transcend or escape time (and space) by riding a magic carpet of sorts that takes you above, beyond, or away from it all for a while. I'm talking about music, television, and videocassettes of movies or special-interest programs. Beyond that, there are audiocassettes—books on tape, "radio theater" productions, environmental sounds for relaxation.

The relaxation created by listening to music is an effective pain-control technique. Music therapy, which uses different types of music for creating different moods and energy dynamics in the body, is a subject of growing interest and research. Appendix H contains suggestions of classical recordings that can inspire and relax you.

Especially for those who have limited use of hands or arms or else who have restricted vision, music and other audio entertainment is a blessing. You may not realize just how available all sorts of audiocassettes and tapes are. Most public libraries will lend out not only the tapes but the cassette players as well. Some will even deliver the items to your home if you have no transportation. (There are, you will find, certain compensations to being temporarily handicapped.) Consult the Resource Guide at the back of the book for a list of tapes and sources.

Television watching is probably the number-one time-escaping activity of the recuperating person, and for good reason. TV is easy. You may be wondering, however, if TV may be helping or actually hindering your healing process. My sister Mia reports that when she is feeling low, TV only intensifies those feelings. Comparing her own condition with the happy, healthy, perfect TV people only makes her more depressed. But when Ray was recuperating from his surgery he found TV to be a welcome friend. Unfortunately, he also found that "the friend wouldn't leave because I wouldn't turn it off. I had to begin a process of weaning myself from the set." If you aren't certain as to just how therapeutic TV is in your own recuperation, ask yourself these questions:

Am I laughing more as a result of what I see on TV?
Do I feel better about myself, about life in general, as a
    result of my TV watching?
Does my pain and self-focus diminish as I watch TV?

If you can answer yes to all of the above, you are probably using TV wisely. If you answered no to any, you may want to consider other time-escaping activities that will promote your health.

I loafe and invite my soul, I lean
and loafe at my ease observing a
spear of summer grass.
WALT WHITMAN, *"Song of Myself"*

Daydreaming. Now there's a much-maligned skill you might want to develop or recultivate. Many of our greatest inventors and scientists were reprimanded for their creative fantasies. Yet the results of such speculation and imagination can be seen gracing the walls of our art museums and flying through clouds in our skies. Recuperation will offer ample opportunity to daydream, so enjoy it.

Mind watching is another habit to be cultivated, since it is an invaluable step in the deeper understanding of who you are. People who learn to watch the mind, almost as if it were a movie, are able to maintain a balance and stability about themselves even when things around them are falling apart. They learn that most fear is really the result of confused thinking. As this thinking is identified, the fear can be turned off or ignored. Taking a journey inside your own mind, watching how one thought leads to another, is the beginning of a long and fascinating adventure that may lead you, as it has led others, to the heart of things. We'll talk more about mind watching in step 7.

And then, of course, there is sleeping. How lucky you are that now it becomes a necessary requirement for your healing! Enjoy your naps, your snoozes, your long, leisurely nights and late mornings. If you have ever been interested in dreams or dreaming, now would be an excellent time to delve into that subject more deeply. You are in a great position to research this field, as you acquire such extensive experience.

A Few Tips on Spending Time

There is no need to apologize for time filling or (heaven help us!) even time wasting while you are in bed. The only criterion for what you do with your time is whether or not it supports you in feeling good about yourself, which means that it will assist your healing. Consider these hints as you plan your use of time:

- Generally, it is not advisable to try heavy reading while you are still in the hospital. Keep the world's problems off your own back for as long as you can. Even reading the newspaper or watching the TV news may expose you to more bad news than you want to hear. Experiment with remaining uninformed for a few days at a time, and learn what that does for your spirits. When "wounded" in any way, you are more susceptible to depressing news than you would be if you were stronger.

- Your energy will last better if you vary your activities and take frequent time-outs. Take five-minute stretch breaks every hour. Take five-minute breathing times, when you do nothing else. Take five to gaze out the window and enjoy the sky. Take five to listen to a favorite piece of music or to make yourself a special cup of tea. Make a five-minute phone call—to encourage someone else, to catch up on news, to share your concerns. Take five minutes to pray. Take five minutes to practice smiling or to laugh or hum. Take five minutes to massage your hands or feet or face. Take a five-minute nap.
- Give yourself permission to do nothing and to enjoy it. The world would be a much better place to live in if more people did nothing now and then, don't you agree? Just think of all the messes that might never have been made, to say nothing of the wars. Doing nothing also conserves energy. It doesn't cost anything. It's even nonfattening.

Make a list of all the advantages of doing nothing. On second thought, forget it. Just do nothing.

Become an Active Partner

> It's supposed to be a professional se-
> cret, but I'll tell you anyway. We doc-
> tors do nothing. We only help and
> encourage the doctor within.
> ALBERT SCHWEITZER

Your relationship with your doctor is critical to your health and recuperation. I learned this the hard way. On a bright January day in 1973, eight months after I was married, I signed over my body to my doctor. The forms I read were cold and clear. I was going in for surgery to find out what was growing in my ovaries. My signature on the documents meant that the doctor could do whatever he thought necessary once he opened me up and had a look. Waking from the operation, I learned that I had had a total hysterectomy. I was twenty-eight years old.

To this day I do not know if this radical surgery was absolutely necessary. I don't burden myself by asking and reasking the question anymore; I put my energy into creating a rich and joyful life with what is, not in wondering about what could have been. But I tell this story often to emphasize how easy it is to assume the role of unquestioning patient, frightened child, or victim in the face of powerful authority figures like doctors or impersonal institutions like hospitals.

My failure to ask questions, my passive acceptance of whatever I was told, served neither myself nor my doctor. I stayed scared, my doctor stayed invulnerable. It is not an uncommon scenario. Many others, women and men, have reported the same thing.

We all give up some responsibility for our lives in big and small ways all the time. We have to. We need other people's help—

to change the oil in the car, to get a decent haircut. We need the advice of specialists sometimes. We definitely need doctors. That is not the problem.

Where we run into trouble is when we become *patients*—a word I would like to eliminate as it is generally used. Because for most people, being a patient is equated with being passive, with giving up their own vote, their own voice in their medical treatment and their life in general. In place of "patient" I would substitute "participant"—or better yet, "partner." Such a simple distinction changes the whole nature of the relationship between you and your doctors and other care givers.

You now have a responsibility to become a player on the team, the healing team—doctors, nurses, family, friends, and you, all pulling together. The modern Chinese sanatorium represents such a place. Patients are requested to keep a diary of notes that describe each phase of their illness. They report signs of returning strength, signs of weakening or relapse. These notes then become a part of the complete medical records of the case, right alongside data compiled by the attending health professionals. This cooperative approach not only builds mutual appreciation among team members but sharpens the self-awareness of the person in treatment, a factor that leads to one's assuming more responsibility for one's own well-being.

ANATOMY OF A PARTNERSHIP

If you were setting up a business, planning to share the risks, responsibilities, and profits with a number of partners, you'd surely be asking questions such as Who is responsible to whom and for what and by when?

Are you asking those questions now—of your doctors and care givers, your family, and yourself? Certainly in establishing a partnership that has your life and health as its business, you will want to be at least as circumspect and thorough as you would be in a financial venture.

Don't be just a patient; be a partner in your recovery. A healing partnership involves four important considerations:

■ Maintaining a positive attitude about yourself and your treatment—a factor that is essentially in your control.

- Creating trust, through mutual respect, cooperation, and communication among yourself, your doctor, and every other member of your healing team.
- Becoming an educated and assertive consumer within the medical establishment—not so much from a legal point of view as from a desire for knowledge and acknowledgment.
- Taking realistic responsibility for your own health without assuming blame.

Begin to consider these now. Make them signposts in your mind. Further details on each consideration can be found in the sections to come.

The Essential Attitude—A Positive One!

Norman Cousins, whose prescriptions for laughter were mentioned in step 1, had a heart attack in 1980. One of his attending physicians at the UCLA School of Medicine describes the remarkable scene of his first view of Cousins in the hospital. "The swinging doors to the emergency room open wide and a rolling stretcher comes through. The patient sits up, waves, grins, and says, 'Gentlemen, I want you to know that you're looking at the darnedest healing machine that's ever been wheeled into this hospital'." That remark epitomizes Cousins' personality, philosophy, and approach to illness and healing.

What Cousins knew was that his positive attitude was his best medicine. And he wanted the whole team to share in it too. His was not to be a silent partnership.

The power of positive attitude in determining how quickly and completely we heal from illness is a topic of great interest today. In his best-selling book, *Love, Medicine and Miracles,* Bernie Siegel, a practicing surgeon and professor at Yale University, chronicles the lessons he has learned about self-healing from his "exceptional patients," those who have refused to give up hope or participate in defeat. As Siegel writes, they "manifest the will to live in its most potent form . . . take charge of their lives . . . work hard to achieve health and peace of mind." What characterizes these exceptional individuals (and Siegel claims we all have this potential) is that they are ready and willing to love themselves and to love life, despite their painful pasts or their current problems. They have faith in themselves. These are the survivors.

This faith in oneself does not magically appear; it is built on the day-to-day acknowledgment of and caring for the body, the mind, the emotions, and the soul. One friend described it as the choice to send "love letters" to herself, even when she felt ugly or sick or weak.

You build a positive attitude and send a love letter to yourself every time you

- affirm your total confidence in your own recovery;
- honor your body's needs for rest and nutrition, clear air, exercise, energizing breath, touch;
- express gratitude to and for your body and its remarkable healing capacity;
- listen to yourself and honor your healing rhythms;
- cultivate your sense of humor and look for the "good news";
- associate with people who uplift you, people with whom you can have nourishing conversations;
- take time for activities that rest you, feed your heart and soul, expand your interests, and demand your creativity;
- plan for a powerful, joyous, and purposeful future for yourself;
- speak words of love and encouragement to others, and especially to yourself; keep negative thought patterns and destructive self-talk to a minimum;
- trust in God, Divine Providence, or whatever it is that you consider your higher power.

These are the things that bring about peace of mind. And peace of mind will send the body a strong message: *Heal!*

What encourages your positive attitude as you are recuperating? You may be amazed at how many simple things you can do to support yourself. Doris, a middle-aged woman, found comfort in the teddy bear she brought to the hospital with her. (Some hospitals now actually supply them for patients who request them.) Fred had his wife bring in home-cooked soups, which did wonders for his spirits. Terry's mobilization was more difficult. Realizing that his negative attitudes were working against him, he began choosing his TV viewing and his visitors with greater care. He selected only those programs that "fed" him, and he invited only those people who perked up his energy. Like Norman Cousins, Terry realized that *his doctor couldn't operate on what he was thinking or feeling about himself.* He accepted that as his own department.

Create Trust with Your Teammates

Would you set up a partnership with someone you didn't trust? Probably not. Yet in matters of health so many people create relationships with their physicians and other care givers based on convenience at best, fear and ignorance at worst. They hand over important decisions about their lives to people they hardly know or may not respect.

Your trust in your doctor is paramount to your healing. In a study at Johns Hopkins University, psychiatrist Jerome Frank found that among the ninety-eight patients he interviewed, all undergoing surgery for detached retinas, those with a high trust in their doctors healed faster than the others. Dr. Bernie Siegel, previously mentioned, is convinced that the relationship in trust of doctor and patient "is more important, in the long run, than any medicine or procedure." Creating trust is a matter of learning to speak up about your rights and then to cooperate with your team.

Speak up. Trust builds as people communicate with one another, sharing their values and belief systems. If you feel that you do not trust your doctor because you do not know him or her very well, that is an excellent place to start from. Sit down with this individual and have a conversation, person to person. Remember, your doctor is not better or more important than you.

If your relationship with your doctor has gone sour, do not be discouraged; it may still be salvageable. Your doctor is not the enemy, unless you make him so. Often a cold or gruff exterior masks a deep insecurity and sense of helplessness. Remembering that your doctor is just another hurting human being can encourage you to approach the relationship in a different way, a way that invites rather than challenges. So speak up if it's worth it to you. Express your desire to build trust, to work together, to even enjoy each other. We do our physicians and care givers a great favor when we join them in taking responsibility for our healing. Treat your doctors as guides, not gods. As much as they may play the role of being the healers, they are not. But they pay a very heavy price for shouldering this burden.

If you anticipate having additional surgery, speak to your surgeon and others on the team beforehand. Express your feelings and your needs. Ask your surgical team to keep the atmosphere in the operating room as relaxed and caring as possible, since this will affect your responses under anesthesia. Ask them to speak *to* you and *about* you encouragingly, as if you were fully conscious. Suggest that they play gentle music in the background. Your body-mind will pick up these positive, life-affirming messages from the surgical environment. An excellent book by Dr. Richard Moss, *How Shall I Live? Transforming Surgery or Any Health Crisis into Greater Aliveness,* addresses this subject in greater depth.

Often people expect their doctor to be a mind reader, so they don't reveal all that they know about their symptoms or medical history. Secretly they may fear that something is seriously wrong, and not speaking about it fully becomes their way of denying it. The fact that a parent had a history of high blood pressure may or may not be relevant to the case at hand, but one way or another it should be communicated, even if the doctor doesn't ask for it. Adopting an "I dare you to diagnose me correctly" position does not encourage a healthy, trusting partnership.

If you can't talk to your doctor honestly, enlist the help of a friend or family member to express your genuine concerns and to make your needs known for you. Sometimes it is easier to get a third party involved, even though that entails an obvious risk in something getting lost in the translation from the doctor to yourself. But such an interim measure may open the door for more direct communication somewhere down the line.

Cooperate with your team. People often complain about the slowness of their recuperation. Yet when asked if they are following their doctor's suggestions—regarding diet, exercise, medication, or whatever—they become easily defensive. "I know I should, but . . ." always ends in a good excuse. But good excuses don't heal wounds, supply necessary nutrients, or provide energy to sluggish systems.

Researcher Barry Blackwell reviewed hundreds of studies of how thoroughly patients followed the treatment plans suggested by their doctors. He found that in over 50 percent of the cases, patients ignored their doctor's recommendations. Why?

For one thing, many treatment plans may simply require more

effort than most of us are used to making in our own behalf. Often the suggested treatment involves a change of behavior or a modification of lifestyle. As a society we are much more inclined to, say, ask for a tranquilizer than we are to practice stress-management exercises, even though the former carry side effects that may include increased anxiety while the latter are virtually harmless. Along the same lines, we will readily eat highly processed foods with little or no nutritive value but then follow this with an expensive vitamin or mineral supplement. We are a culture that likes pills for our ills.

At other times people do not cooperate with their doctor's instructions because they don't exactly know what is expected and are afraid to ask. Doctors, like the rest of us, often fall short of clear, open communication. Incomplete or poorly explained instructions are commonplace. (You probably know a few jokes, as I do, about suppositories being swallowed rather than inserted and birth control pills being inserted rather than swallowed.) As an active, cooperating participant you will often have to take the initiative here. Ask for a step-by-step rundown of your treatment plan. Request that this be written down for you. Ask for clear explanations of what the problem is, what caused it, how you can prevent it from recurring, and what you can do to learn more about your condition.

If the medical terms used are confusing or frightening to you, ask for an explanation. One of the ways that distance and mistrust are created between partners is that one party holds privileged, "magic" information couched in scientific jargon and the other doesn't. Patients often fail to ask for explanations because they feel small and insignificant.

While we have been focusing primarily on the doctor-patient relationship, there are admittedly many others on your healing team. The same honest sharing, compassionate understanding, and trust building needs to be established with your family members and friends as well.

Assert Your Rights—Be an Informed Consumer

In all this, however, do keep in mind that cooperation with your treatment does not mean blind obedience. If you disagree with your treatment plan, communicate this to your doctor. If your doctor suggests a plan that is impractical for you, discuss it. Come to some understanding with each other. Usually many more options are available than are immediately apparent. Explore alternatives. Accepting treatment recommendations passively and then resisting them actively is a waste of your precious time and effort.

There can be no lasting healing without the cooperation and effort of the patient. Anyone who thinks the doctor is going to do everything for him is in for a sad disappointment.

EVARTS G. LOOMIS AND
J. SIG PAULSEN, *Healing for Everyone*

When we are sick or weak, it is easy to take the line of least resistance. Unfortunately, that may equate with passivity when it comes to getting what we may be entitled to or what we need. Most hospitals have patient advocacy programs to assist you in areas beyond your expertise. But generally our complaints with the medical establishment are easily remedied by basic education and the practice of simple, assertive communication.

As a responsive and responsible partner, you have the right to the following:

- A clear explanation of any recommended procedures. Ask your doctor to use simple language and provide illustrations if necessary.
- A second or even third opinion. In fact, many insurance companies now require this.
- Information about alternative treatments, surgery, or drugs. A single problem can be dealt with in any number of ways. Don't assume you have to go along automatically with everything your physician suggests.
- Knowledge of the possible side effects of your prescribed drugs. A *PDR—Physicians' Desk Reference*—will give you most of the data you need. Ask to see it.

- A lead shield to protect other parts of the body (particularly ovaries or testes) when X-rays are being taken.
- A change of doctors if you are dissatisfied, unhappy, or just not connecting.
- A generic drug prescription, usually less expensive than a brand name.
- Anything that will provide you with greater privacy or comfort.
- Expression of displeasure and inconvenience at being made to wait, or for any other annoyance that seems to be below a reasonable standard of operation of your health professionals.
- Treatment as an adult and an equal human being by everyone—your doctor, nurses, office staff, and so on. Unprofessional treatment, such as condescending or critical language, does not have to be tolerated. Say so.
- Knowledge about your doctor's previous experience in dealing with a condition similar to your own.
- Questioning of authority, not because you want to make points against them but because you want to learn from their expertise. Ask questions about everything and anything. Keep exercising your right to know, your right to decide for yourself.

Remember: This is your body. You know yourself better than anyone else does. Moment to moment, your body is signaling your brain, and vice versa, asking for what it needs and wants. So start tuning into these cues, start honoring them and expressing them. Sharing with your doctors and care givers what you know to be true about your body and what you need for your recuperation establishes you as a valuable cooperating partner, an active participant in your own healing.

Take Responsibility for Yourself

When Phil was in the critical stages of his treatment, he felt completely out of control. "I didn't have my life as I had known it. That was the hardest thing to accept," he admitted. He also offered one of the best definitions ever for recuperation: the period of slowly taking back responsibility for your own life. All the drugs in the world, all the surgery or intervention treatments available, are secondary to the sacred choice that each of us has to make—to support our own healing. Because we can actually *decide* to help heal ourselves, to help ourselves be well. Time and again this will to live has shown itself as the primary factor in determining who merely survives and who genuinely thrives.

The will to live means taking responsibility for all of you. Since you may have to deal with professionals who treat you as if you are not responsible, or with institutions that have been built on this premise, you may be challenged to stand up for your wholeness. Your vision, too, may be clouded by the perception that you are simply an ailing body in need of fixing. It is going to take courage and persistence to keep reminding yourself and every member of your team that you are a whole person. It is going to take attention to keep all of you moving and to assert your will to live.

For some of us, the toughest part of being active participants will be to give up claims to being innocent bystanders or victims of circumstance where our illness or accident is concerned. While it may be true that other social, biological, or environmental factors played a part in our situation, we can look hard at our own choices in the matter and recognize that our choices have power.

Consciously, I certainly didn't want to break my leg skiing. But I did choose to venture out on the slopes without adequately checking my equipment on that particular day. The night Jerry broke up with his girlfriend, he was extremely upset but chose to drive to work anyway—and "accidentally" landed the car in a ditch. Don didn't welcome the massive ruptured aneurysm that laid him up for six months, but for years he had chosen to continue his stress-producing habits despite his doctor's warning. To believe that heart attack, cancer, arthritis—whatever—just "happens" is to deny the profound privilege and responsibility we humans share with other people and with the environment in the creation of our own lives.

Self-responsibility motivates self-understanding and leads to lasting, positive change. If we accept that our choices work in setting the stage for our accidents and illnesses, we acknowledge that they can work every bit as powerfully in taking the stage down, in moving us toward healing. And that is exactly what you are doing in reading this book. Choosing to practice the fine art of recuperation is choosing to heal.

Responsibility never means blame. (As often as I draw that distinction with myself and others, I am amazed at how easily it becomes confused.) With blame we berate ourselves for having done something "bad" or "wrong." We see ourselves as weak or ignorant or stupid. And these self-definitions act as siphons in our vital parts, draining us of energy. With responsibility, however, we increase our energy. We accept our role in the situation for what it is, without beating ourselves up for it. The self-responsible partner uses past mistakes to create new possibilities in life.

Responsibility doesn't mean doing it all yourself, either. The responsible participant is neither the victim who blames himself or others nor the saint who smiles heroically and refuses any kind of help in her healing process. The responsible participant is a flesh-and-blood human being who tries and fails sometimes, tries and succeeds sometimes. Taking responsibility for yourself means keeping a balance by telling the truth about what you can expect from and do for yourself, and what you need to ask from others. The table on the following page lists the characteristics of three different types of patients.

ASKING FOR WHAT YOU NEED— AND GETTING IT

Partners help each other out when they can. But asking for help is not always easy. Getting just what you want from the other members of your healing team, and getting it just when you want it, is not always possible. Pete's accident showed him just how difficult it was for him to ask for help. "I vacillated between being helpless, feeling sorry for myself, and demanding help with everything on the one hand and being stubbornly independent and not asking for help even when I really needed it on the other. It was a constant struggle between dependency and rugged individualism." Some of this struggle comes from denial. Some comes from fear of burdening others or being disappointed in not getting the help that is needed.

By asserting yourself in a caring way, you have a much better chance and will have an easier time. Caring assertiveness is the direct expression of your thoughts and feelings in a way that clearly states your needs while acknowledging the needs and feelings of the other. The following crash course should prove helpful:

What Does It Mean to Be an Active Partner?

The Victim: The "Poor" Patient	*The Saint: The "Perfect" Patient*	*The Responsible Participant*
Blames others, outside forces—anything	Blames self	Realistically confronts what is
Complains: "Poor me . . ." "Yes, but . . ."	Resigned to fate or punishment	Accepts responsibility
Resents others, especially their health or good fortune	Plays brave, strong, cheerful, sweet, or holy	Tells the truth, moment to moment
Bitter	Doesn't ask directly for needs	Avoids blaming self or others
Serious	Guilty, but won't share this	Assumes control as much as possible
Gives up easily	Rationalizes for the behavior of others	Asks directly for needs
Doesn't ask for needs directly	Sees no alternatives	Expresses emotions readily—the whole range
Sees no alternatives	Serious	Looks for humor, fun, play
Sees condition as bad luck	Tries to handle it all, to keep everything under control	Takes risks
Self-indulgent	Unwilling to share true feelings	Keeps open to all alternatives
Takes no responsibility	Doesn't need support	Participates in the healing process
Increases self-destructive behaviors		Asks questions
Doesn't trust support		Establishes a support system
		Looks for the learning in everything

Lesson 1: Do not apologize for needing help. You deserve help, you deserve caring, you deserve understanding—not because you've earned it, but simply because you are a member of the family, the human family. Human beings are allowed to be sick, weak, to make mistakes, to have accidents, and to ask for help. People need one another—and want to help one another. Your visitors and care givers will appreciate *direct requests* much more than your apologetic supplications.

Lesson 2: Keep an ongoing list. In your journal or in your head, keep track of anything you think of that will make your recuperation easier and more joyful. This may include anything from a candy bar to a computer, any service from a back rub to a room remodeling. Questions to ask your doctor? Make a list and use it. It is easy to "forget" your concerns or to lose courage to ask about them. Writing them down (ask someone to do this for you if you can't write yet) makes it harder to dismiss them.

Lesson 3: Listen. Do not let any vague offer of assistance pass you by. Be immediately ready to take someone up on an offer to help. You will be amazed at how often someone will. If you are not getting what you need, it may be because you are letting your embarrassment or your mistrust get the better of you. It's your own fault! Listen:

> *Visitor* (stepping out the door): If there's anything I can do to help, please don't hesitate to ask.

> *You:* I'm so glad you asked. There is something I really would appreciate right away.

Lesson 4: Be direct and honest. First, state what you need. Second, make your request in straight, simple language. Third, say when you want it. Suppose that it is difficult for you to get out of bed and you want to have your hair washed. You might say, for example: *(What you need)* "Mary, I need my hair washed." *(The direct request)* "Will you do it for me?" *(When you want it)* "Can you do it tomorrow morning about nine?"

This specific and direct approach is really the most considerate. A vague request like "Can you do something for me?" makes your visitor feel cornered and doesn't get you what you need. Offering a preferred or definite time also helps everyone: You have taken charge; your guest knows what is needed and expected. Furthermore, there's a better chance the task will be completed!

Lesson 5: Respect (and expect an occasional) no. If you are not willing to be honestly refused your request, don't bother asking. Your visitor or care giver has the right to be unable to come through for you at this time.

Lesson 6: Be truthful with yourself about what you need. Use your requests honestly to get what you need, not as tests or trials to prove if somebody loves you or not. On the other hand, if your need is urgent, don't be afraid to communicate that urgency as strongly as you can. The words *This is an emergency* will not be dismissed lightly.

Lesson 7: If you don't know what you want, say what you feel. Often you will not know exactly what it is you want or need. All you know is that you feel terribly confused, or scared, or helpless. Express that, and simply ask for help. For example: "I am so scared right now. I don't know what to do. Can you help?" Now at least the door is open. You don't have to endure all by yourself.

Lesson 8: Be persistent. Just because one person may refuse a request does not mean that everybody will. Just because a helper says no today does not necessarily mean no forever. Don't give up on your helpers, your doctor, or yourself.

Lesson 9: Be appreciative. Express sincere gratitude for any kindness shown you. Do not demand or even expect anything, but do appreciate everything. When others are genuinely acknowledged for their service, they are likely to want to give more.

Lesson 10: Be smart; know what help is available. If you need help of any kind and can't get it from those around you, get it from anywhere you can. Service agencies, religious organizations, local hospitals, crisis information centers . . . it doesn't matter who you call first. The important thing is to start calling and find out what assistance is available to you. It is always easier to suffer in silence than it is to ask for help. Be smart. Check appendix I for more information on support networks and services.

THE MIDDLE PATH

The fine art of recuperation is like a path of balance that winds its way around the extremes whenever possible. And while some people will need to do more to become active participants on the healing team, others may be well advised to do less.

When Andy, a former colleague, called me recently, he was quite distraught. "There are so many different nutritional programs to follow; I'm overwhelmed! What if I choose the wrong one? How do I know that the one I'm following is the best? One doctor tells me one thing, another recommends something else. Or maybe it's not nutrition that I should focus on. Maybe I need to look for a new therapist, or go back to church, or . . ."

This is not untypical. Many of us become obsessed with our recovery and frightened of our responsibility to the point where we cause ourselves more stress. We can drive ourselves crazy trying to keep up with every suggestion about some great new therapy that's been mentioned to us.

Active participation may mean doing some reading, some questioning, some investigating of alternatives. But do it from a secure foundation, the way some folks find themselves a better job. They don't quit the one they have until the new one is assured. So, too, as you study and inform yourself of your options, as you sensitize yourself to what your body needs and knows, avoid throwing everything out and starting from scratch. Keep to your suggested regimen as you stay open to a better one.

I am utterly convinced that exact diet or exercise or regimen of any kind is not nearly as important as an overall mental and emotional state of well-being. Focus on keeping your balance as you become an active participant, and the rest will be a lot easier.

*So sometimes things are ahead
and sometimes they are behind;
Sometimes breathing is hard,
sometimes it comes easily;
Sometimes there is strength and
sometimes weakness;
Sometimes one is up and sometimes
down.
Therefore the sage avoids extremes,
excesses, and complacency.*

LAO TSU, *Tao Te Ching*, #29,
[edited by Gia-Fu Feng,
translation by Jane English]

Help Your Visitors to Be Well

> Issue an invitation. Ask your family
> and friends to stop socializing and, in-
> stead, to open their hearts. . . . They
> may open themselves to you by telling
> you how frustrated they feel because
> they don't know how to help you.
> Whatever you both say and do, such
> honesty and love can unite you in the
> moment. There is more energy in this
> than in hiding or pretending to be
> cheerful and positive.
> RICHARD MOSS, *How Shall I Live?*

It is almost impossible to recuperate alone. Even
though you might like nothing better than to disappear completely
while you heal, you probably can't. So you might as well face up
to it: Your illness, weakness, or disease is going to affect other
people. Like you, those close by are going to be grieving a loss—
the loss of you in some ways, the loss of their illusions about your
invulnerability, the loss of their time, their plans, or even their
money. Knowing this will help you to be with them in healthy ways,
ways that allow you and them to learn, to love, to laugh, and to
heal.

VISITORS: A MIXED BLESSING

Like so many other things in life, having visitors when you are
recuperating has its plusses and its minuses. Visitors can be your
salvation from the long, open hours with nothing much to do.
They can brighten your life, especially if they are genuinely caring

people. A child's laughter and innocence, for instance, may feed you more nourishment in a few minutes than hours of serious adult companionship. Visitors can do for you what you cannot do for yourself, by providing a willing ear for listening, a shoulder for you to cry on, a remembrance of your connection to a wider family of humanity.

And then, on the other hand . . . there are times when your visitors will seem more trouble than they're worth. Their pain and their problems may intensify your own. Other people may grate on your nerves more than usual. They may seem uncaring and selfish, concerned only with themselves. They may be such "professional helpers" that you are left feeling like a guinea pig or a therapy client with all the unasked-for advice they give you. Face it: Some of your visitors are going to be a lot sicker than you in some ways. The challenge and the potential gift in this step of the fine art of recuperation is that in helping your visitors to be well, you help yourself—both now and for the future. Building a support system of honest, caring friends and helpers is a way of healing and an assurance of ongoing health.

When social contact is increased or loneliness reduced, the immune system seems to strengthen. A group of thirty elderly people in retirement homes showed increased immune competence in terms of both NK (natural killer) cells and antibodies from being visited three times a week for a month.

BLAIR JUSTICE, *Who Gets Sick*

The Good News About Your Illness

The following compensations for being ill can also guide you in helping your visitors to be well.

People like to help one another. Just recall how many service organizations you've heard about, and you will have a slight appreciation for how much we want to serve and support one another. Now that you are in need, you will give your friends and family a way to feel more useful in their own lives. Your illness, weakness, and dependency gives people a chance to show their love. There is always the possibility of a deeper bonding between yourself and the person who visits and cares for you. Your illness provides that opportunity for your friends and family.

Your presence gets people thinking. Without doing a thing, you will be inviting your visitors to do some hard thinking about their own lives and to be more appreciative of what they have. You are a living lesson.

You get to share your wisdom. The common assumption is that pain and hardship builds strength and inner wisdom. People may be inclined to listen to you more respectfully, hoping that you have something valuable to offer. And you very well may. Maybe your situation has afforded you some sharpened insight. You have, perhaps, been looking your old priorities squarely in the face in a way that your more active friends have been avoiding. Maybe now you are less inclined to "sweat the small stuff," or perhaps your tolerance for "beating around the bush" has plummeted to near zero.

Because you are a captive audience, people will also tell you their problems or share their concerns. They will perceive you as safe because you are hurting, as they are. I always liked this part of being sick, this opportunity to be a "wounded healer," to lend my willing ear to others in pain. If this is something you enjoy, do it. If, on the other hand, you find that some people just want to use you as a place to dump their complaints, tell them clearly that you can't handle any more than your own right now.

You are granted more leeway for just being yourself. What might normally have annoyed other people about you may be more readily forgiven now. After all, you're recuperating! And those things that others previously appreciated about you may be even more appreciated now. After all, you're recuperating! You will probably be allowed a few extra tears, even by those who were previously uncomfortable with emotional expression. You will probably be excused for speaking about your fears, even by those who are more fearful than yourself. In short, you may be given permission to be a human being.

You will have a fine chance to play out your unconventional or silly self and be applauded for it. If this disturbs other people, they will blame it on your condition. So have fun and capitalize on this advantage.

You might get some good presents. Flowers, books, cards, phone calls— don't undervalue a single one of them. Anyone who takes the time to send you a greeting or a gift is expressing their caring for and connection with you in some way. You mean something to them. You can appreciate yourself for that.

The More Difficult News

Here are some caveats in dealing with your visitors:

People grieve and heal in their own good time. George was out of the hospital and recovering with enthusiasm while his wife, Nancy, was feeling more depressed as the days went on. Prior to his surgery they had been inseparable, a total support system for each other. What Nancy found later was that she had not faced her own grief while she was encouraging George through his. He, on the other hand, had faced the terror of his condition and had come to some peace about it. He had done a lot more anticipatory grieving.

This is a common occurrence, especially with spouses. Since we each have our own rhythms, we can't expect that those we live with and those we love will necessarily grieve or heal at the same rate as ourselves. Your spouse or primary care giver may also often feel like a second-class citizen, even if it is not admitted to you. When Fred was recuperating from a kidney transplant, his wife, Pam, reported that she was getting little or no personal acknowledgment from others. Every phone call, every person she met immediately asked: "How's Fred?" She began to wonder if anybody cared about how *she* was holding up. Keep this in mind and support your spouse or primary care giver with your own thanks. Ask your visitors to remember them too.

Sickness makes people uncomfortable. Hospitals or sickrooms are awkward environments. The rules for how to be a good visitor are not clearly defined. People are afraid—that's basic. If you keep this in mind, you will save yourself and them a lot of unnecessary discomfort.

Frank reported that people seemed to walk on eggshells around him after his surgery. "Some people just didn't know how to act. It's like they'd hang out near the door to see if I was still me. And this was hard for me at first. They'd hide their sense of humor, and that's what I probably needed the most."

Even if you never say a word, your very presence reminds people who see you or hear about you that "It could happen to me," and people may avoid getting too close to you for just this reason. It's as if you were contagious. When faced with the reality of disability or confinement, people get nervous and sometimes lose their social equilibrium.

Guilt abounds. Friends and casual visitors—and your family in particular—may feel guilty when they are with you. Maybe you disrupted their lives and they are feeling angry about it, but they can't admit it to you. After all, what can *you* do about it? You just got sick. So instead your family may turn the anger in upon themselves, and it will show up as guilt. Or they will replay their life experiences with you and remember how many times they didn't help you or express their love for you. Now that you are down, they feel remorse. It's the old story of not appreciating what we've got until it is gone. They may feel responsible. They will fantasize that perhaps they could have prevented this from happening to you or perhaps have warned you in some way.

If you are lonely and hurting, you may be tempted to feed this guilt in others so that you get more attention. Be careful. This type of interaction has a way of backfiring. Avoid taking advantage of somebody else's guilt. You can get what you need in direct ways, as we've discussed in step 4. You may want to refer back to that section now as a reminder.

Helplessness creates anxiety. The nervousness that you observe in people around you often has to do with their feelings of helplessness. You know it, they know it. This helpless feeling will sometimes express itself in anger, sometimes in withdrawal, sometimes in guilt, sometimes in oversolicitous activity around you. Be ready for all and any of it. And once again, try to keep your sense of humor, as a deaf friend who was traveling called upon himself to do. As he was getting his seat assignment for a plane trip, he handed the ticket agent a note that read: "I am hearing impaired." The agent immediately became flustered and left her post. In a few minutes she returned—with a wheelchair!

Remember, there is more social acceptance for physical illness than there is for the emotional problems that may accompany it. The more physically apparent our ailments, the more direct ways others can help us deal with them. So if your problem is depression, people will have a tougher time knowing what to do for you than if you had a broken leg. And their sense of helplessness might discourage them from paying you a visit, or even calling you.

You are a shooting star. You may notice a sharp drop-off in attention following the crisis phase of illness. You were special for a while. Even new people, such as those you met in the hospital or in treatment, involved themselves with you for a time. But now the world is fast resuming for these others, even though for you it remains stalled. The visits get shorter or stop altogether; the demands start piling up again. The same people who were overly solicitous of you in the beginning may seem to turn away, leaving you feeling more alone and lonely than ever, a sort of shooting star across their sky.

Living the fine art of recuperation will require personal strength to accept aloneness, to generate compassion for yourself from yourself, and to understand that other people are doing only the best they can.

And now that you are better acquainted with both what advantages may be in store for you and also what to watch out for, you'll be better able to benefit from the following suggestions geared toward increasing both your visitors' well-being and, by extension, your own.

FIRST AID FOR YOUR VISITORS

Show the Visitor Your Positive Attitude

You may have to encourage family and visitors to keep their sense of humor around you. And it is worth the effort, since their attitudes and energy are going to affect you. The following signs posted on your door might help set the desired tone:

NO PITY PLEASE
I'M ACTUALLY BETTER OFF IN MANY WAYS THAN YOU ARE!

NO SMOKING, NO GUILT, NO PESTS, NO MORE BAD NEWS,
AND NO BORROWING MY DRUGS

PLEASE SPARE ME ANY STORIES OF SOMEBODY WHO IS
WORSE OFF THAN I AM. WHEN YOU VISIT THEM YOU PROB-
ABLY SAY THE SAME THING, AND USE ME AS AN EXAMPLE.

PRICE OF ADMISSION: YOUR FAVORITE JOKE.
TELL IT TO ME NOW!

SHARE YOUR STRENGTH—HOLD ME

CONSERVE HOSPITAL SPACE—GET IN BED WITH ME

VISITORS ARE KINDLY REQUESTED TO REFRAIN FROM REFER-
ENCES TO THE FOLLOWING:
   THE FUNERAL ARRANGEMENTS BEING MADE FOR THE PATIENT
      . . . JUST IN CASE.
   HOW NICE IT IS AT THE OFFICE NOW THAT THE PATIENT IS
      AWAY.
   WHOM YOU SAW OUT WITH THE PATIENT'S HUSBAND (OR WIFE)
      LAST NIGHT.
   ALL THOSE SILLY LITTLE OVERSIGHTS THAT OCCUR IN
      SURGERY, IN DRUG PRESCRIPTION, AND IN BILLING.

Now go ahead and make up your own list of visitors' rules.
And don't forget to post them.

Disarm Your Visitor with Honesty

I assume that you want your visitors to be well and that you want
them around because they *care* about you, not because they feel
obliged to be there. I assume you want their love, not their pity,
and that you want them to act naturally, even playfully, with you
if possible—that you want them to drop any feelings of guilt because they may not be able to help you.

But this may not be easy to do. Remember, you cannot change anybody else. If people around you want to feel bad, guilty, or angry, they will. While their feelings can be loosened up and lightened by your addressing them directly, what often happens instead is that you and they carry on a game of mutual pretense: *I hurt and you know it. You hurt and I know it. But let's not ever mention it.* That kind of communication is rarely satisfying. The stress of having to monitor every thought, word, or action for fear of making somebody uncomfortable is a heavy burden for you or your visitor to bear.

I support the use of disarming honesty as a way of helping yourself and your visitors to be well. By "disarming," I mean the honesty that surprises the other into dropping defenses and masks. Telling the truth is what it's all about, and you are the one who needs to make the first move. An effective formula involves four simple steps: reporting, reassuring, requesting, encouraging. Here's how to put them into action:

Report: Start by simply telling what you see, hear, or feel.

Example: "Henry, you look more concerned about me than I am about myself."

Reassure: Try to put your visitors at ease. Share with them that discomfort is natural and that you are aware of it.

Example: "Everybody feels nervous and a little bit artificial around me at this time."

Request: Say what you want. Express your desire to move beyond the discomfort, the guilt, the fear.

Example: "I want to be myself with you, and I want you to be yourself around me."

Encourage: Urge others to share their feelings with you.

Example: "Tell me what's going on with you, what you're feeling."

You have now offered your visitor an invitation, a hand to hold, so to speak. Clearing the air in this way allows everyone to breathe easier, and it can prepare you all to share a few good laughs.

Invite Silence

A friend is one with whom we can be silent and still feel at home, close, and connected. In fact, sometimes silence is more conducive to getting to know someone than is the noisy chatter of voices speaking of inconsequential things. Visitors can tire you by demanding responses to questions on topics in which you have no interest.

Invite silence. There are many ways to do that. Ask your visitor to simply hold your hand and pray silently with you. Suggest that your visitor breathe with you as a way of relaxing your own stress (use one of the breathing exercises suggested in appendix C). When done together with someone, these pursuits' effects are magnified and provide healing all around. Whatever you can suggest that will lessen your visitor's stress will lessen your own, too.

Put Your Visitor to Work on the Spot

If conversation is tiresome or your visitor uncomfortable, ask if he would like to do something for you. If the answer is yes, suggest *several* possibilities so that he can choose whatever feels easiest to do. Ask to be read to, especially from an inspirational book that will encourage the visitor as much as yourself. If you feel particularly trusting, ask for a back rub or foot massage. Suggest that some relaxing music accompany this endeavor. Recommend a game you might play together—a card game, a puzzle.

Is your room a bit dusty or musty? Request that a window be opened or the shelves be dusted off; perhaps your books could be arranged or the floor swept. Giving your visitors specific tasks will make them feel useful and give you something to talk about other than the weather.

Check your mental list of the jobs to be done that you are unable to handle as you recuperate. Maybe you're concerned that the car needs washing, or the books need to go back to the library, or the lawn needs cutting. You'll be amazed how close you both can get by sharing in the work together.

Set a Time Limit

Often people will refrain from visiting because they are afraid it will take up too much of their time, that they might be expected to sit around for hours. If you can assure your visitors that even a few minutes are greatly appreciated, they may be more inclined to turn those few minutes into precious "quality time" with you. When someone calls asking to see you or else drops by unexpectedly, you can simply say, "I'd be so happy to have you visit; just understand that I may need to rest or sleep frequently." Then if you or your visitor is uncomfortable, your need to rest will generally be respected.

Change the Subject

Have a list of topics of interest to you, or else interesting questions that may involve both of you in subjects that lift your spirits. After telling the story of my accident to everybody who called or visited, I soon got terribly bored—so I told my friends as much. You might want to reduce your narrative to a few sentences and suggest, honestly, that you'd much rather talk about something else—whatever it may be!

Make your guests the topic of conversation. Ask about *their* lives. Ask about what's going on in the world outside—neighborhood news, church news, news at the job. Or ask for favorite jokes or other bits of humor they may have come across recently. Ask what they would do with their time if they had as much of it as you. Ask whom they'd like to have in the bed next to them if they were in a hospital for six months. Ask them to tell you a dream or a wish they have. Ask them what they would take with them if they could bring only three things along on a move to an outer-space colony. You get the idea.

TO THE VISITOR OR CARE GIVER

Since the health and well-being of your visitors and care givers will influence your own, this section is provided as a reminder to them. Read it over yourself first if you like, and then hand them the book.

Encourage them to read it through, and let them know how much you appreciate their time, love, and help.

In helping the other grow I do not impose my own direction; rather, I allow the direction of the other's growth to guide what I do.
MILTON MAYEROFF, *On Caring*

Almost everyone who cares for the sick or visits a recuperating friend or relative gets to share in the stress of their condition. We human beings who are so good at responding to crises with one another often neglect to keep ourselves healthy in the process. Your well-being and positive attitude are among the most important gifts you can give to the other.

Tell the truth. That means do what you can, and gently and firmly say what you cannot do. Avoid being a martyr. Your friend will feel this, and you may end up being resentful because you haven't been truthful.

Don't put on a show to prove your good attitude. A positive attitude is essentially an inside job. *Be* positive, and it will emanate from all over you. If on some days you are exceptionally low, stay home. Visit on days when you have a bit of energy to spare. If you must visit anyway, or if you are a primary care giver, report that your energy is down, and ask your recuperating team member to avoid taking it personally.

Don't take anything personally. Your friend or relative is necessarily self-centered because of his or her situation. He needs to be focused on himself to give as much energy as possible to his healing. But that may mean that he will be less sensitive to your feelings and overly sensitive to everything else. Develop the skill of brushing off little "hurts," those remarks that sound as if your help is not appreciated. Create in your imagination a clear plastic shield that will protect you from getting stung. Remember that grief brings up many strong and strange emotions, and your friend or relative may be having a rough time dealing with these newfound feelings. You may be an unsuspecting target.

Take extra care of your own health. Your schedule may be disrupted by the accident or illness, and that may incline you to eat more junk food, drink more coffee, neglect to exercise or relax. During times of family stress (and you're evidently a part of the family if you're reading this), it is more important than ever to keep your own health in focus. Remember, you can't give what you do not have. Boost your own energy reserves and you'll have more to spend. In appendix C of this book you will find numerous stress-reduction exercises that you can practice on your own or, even better, with your recuperating partner.

Keep renewing your own sense of humor. Whatever it takes to animate your own laughter and good humor will be rewarded many times over when you share this with the healing person. Find jokes or joke books, funny records or tapes to play. Check TV listings for really humorous movies or shows, get a VCR and a classic comedy movie and watch it together. Look for the good news all around you and report on that when you are visiting.

Do something! Look for tangible ways to assist your friend or relative. Ask specifically for what is wanted and needed. Cook a meal. Run errands. Offer to give a foot rub, back rub, or a massage. (Instructions for massaging can be found in appendix E.) Keeping yourself active will help you avoid accumulating the stress that comes with feeling helpless.

Don't do something! Recognize that the most valuable help you may give to someone else is just your silent, listening presence. Be there for the other. Drop your own agendas for what *you* may think is best, and listen between the lines for what is really being asked. So often a healing person requires only a few minutes of quiet companionship and perhaps a hand to hold. "Less is more" is a good guideline to follow here. Sharpening your sensitivity to what the other desires instead of imposing what you think will do the most good is charity of the highest order.

Be responsible for yourself, and let the recuperating person be responsible for himself or herself. It is not your job to guarantee that the patient is always entertained, nor to solve his or her problems. You have your own life to live and need not apologize or feel guilty about that. And besides, if you take over more than you should, you will be robbing the other of the one thing that is most needed—a sense of control over her own life.

Some patients seem to demand oversolicitousness. Don't buy it. Others will resent any assistance. Back off, but don't disappear. Give the healing person plenty of privacy. Encourage him to resume control as soon—and as much—as possible. Anything you can do to foster this reclaiming of control will be worthwhile. Perhaps a phone hooked up in the sickroom would do it, or maybe you simply need to consult with the patient about a choice of menu. Be straightforward about it. Have an open conversation in which you brainstorm together the many ways that you can aid in their asserting control of their lives again.

Allow the full expression of feelings. Listen to complaints, fears, and insecurities without amplifying them. In other words, just allow. Avoid judgment or moralizing of any kind. (Even advice should be kept to a minimum.) Watch your own tendencies to stop the expression of tears or anger. Remember that your partner or friend is grieving a loss of personal freedom, and the liberty to let go of emotional baggage is vitally important at this time. Let yourself cry with him or her if you care to. Not only will this support your own health, it will deepen the bond of trust that is growing between the two of you.

Be a participant, but not a rescuer. If necessary, you can serve as an advocate or intermediary between the patient and the doctor or hospital or other care givers. You may want to inform yourself about the illness or alternative modes of treatment. You may want to study ways to improve care-giving at home. A local visiting nurses' association is an excellent resource in this domain. Avoid becoming a crusader, or you may end up only increasing your own stress. Be an informed consumer, and share what you are learning with your recuperating friend—if he or she wants you to take on this role. Here, as in every other aspect of participation, ask first!

Above all, remember that your support and participation will be greatly appreciated.

Turn the Crisis into an Opportunity

> The skill of being fully alive does not
> lie in expertly avoiding crisis; crisis is
> not usually avoidable. Rather, healthy
> living seems to involve meeting with
> problems in such a way that some-
> thing of value is learned.
>
> NAOMI REMEN, *The Human Patient*

You are now well under way to understanding the fine art of recuperation. But there is more. With certain approaches, you can go beyond mere recovery to true recuperation, beyond coping to creating, beyond surviving to thriving.

At age thirty-eight, Jack had a heart attack. Six years later he is still adamant: "It was the best thing that ever happened to me." When I asked him to elaborate, he continued:

My career was everything to me, and I was hot stuff. At thirty-one I was the director of management consulting for a major accounting firm—the youngest person ever to hold that position, I might add. And because I deserved it I had no qualms about bragging of my records—like closing thirty-seven bond deals in one year. I was a whiz kid, and I was paying a high price for it—smoking, never exercising, stressed all the time! On a scale of one to ten, my stress level was a twelve. Then my heart attack changed all that forever. I stopped smoking for good. I started exercising at least three times a week. I learned how to say no to outside demands and began saying yes to myself—which was probably the biggest single change of my life. I even adopted a new religion. All in all, I made a commitment to myself and to improving the quality of my life. And you know, it's paid off. My life is terrific now, and I'm convinced it can only get better.

Just before we finished talking recently, Jack lowered his voice as if sharing a secret: "It sounds awful to say, but I really wish some of my friends would have just a little heart attack so they would wake up to the craziness of their lives the way I did."

Jack took a life-threatening crisis and turned it into a life-transforming gift. It wasn't easy. It didn't happen overnight. And he was no Pollyanna about the process. Jack's decisions took courage and patience, honesty and hard work—more than he'd ever allowed himself before. He made a decision to live again, but sanely this time. And that is what he is doing today.

So did Rob, a young doctor who underwent surgery and treatment for cancer back in 1978. His health crisis inspired him to launch HealthMark Program for Life, a nutrition-and-exercise program that today has thousands of participants. "I always wondered what my life would have been had that not happened and changed everything." Rob is now a triathlete who bicycles to work and runs in marathons to celebrate his freedom from cancer.

Darla, a former student and research assistant, used her crisis—a case of postpolio muscle atrophy—to propel her into new dimensions of self-understanding and spiritual growth. Months of painful struggle culminated in acceptance, and with that acceptance she began to heal. "I've come a long way," she wrote to me recently. "I'm getting excited just thinking about how much more there is to learn and do and be. I set out in a canoe headed down a creek. The creek has become a river now, with new and wider vistas than any I'd seen before. And I am grateful for all that has brought me to the wonderful and beautiful place I am now." Darla's experience in healing herself led her to write a book in which she shares with others the tools she developed for herself.

OPPORTUNITY KNOCKS

It does sound awful to wish a "little heart attack" on a friend, but when you've seen somebody hit bottom, lose everything, and then turn around as a result, it blurs the usual distinctions between blessing and curse. In fact, the Chinese ideogram for "cri-

CRISIS
IS

机 危

Danger

and

Opportunity

sis" is a combination of the ideograms for "danger" and "opportunity."

Up until now we have focused on balancing the danger aspects of crisis, addressing areas of immediate need: how to face the fact of your loss, how to give your body what it needs to heal, how to handle strong and strange emotions, how to fill your time with something other than worry. Most of these techniques have concentrated on basic stress management. You will continue to work in these areas throughout your recuperation. At the same time, you're probably growing in your awareness that possibilities await beyond simple maintenance. Like Jack, you may be recognizing an opportunity in disguise—a chance to reassess and realign and recommit yourself to life and health in a deeper way. This realization won't necessarily make you feel happy or optimistic. Quite the contrary; it may be extremely tough to consider.

Few would argue that pain can be a powerful teacher. But who wants it? There's not much fun in being sick. Crisis shocks your system. Flat on your back, in pain, scared, frustrated, there's scant comfort in the option of this "great opportunity" that may be available to you. All you want is to feel better so you can resume the business of living a normal life again. And you should. Resistance to pain and discomfort is natural.

So I'm not suggesting that you enjoy it. But I do urge you to *use it for all it's worth.* Whether you like it or not, your life is never going to be exactly the same as it was before this illness or accident. You are being changed by what you are going through. You can't prevent it; that's simply the nature of life. Whether you are ultimately wiser, stronger, healthier, and happier as a result of all this is *your choice now.*

Define Your Life for Yourself

I have seen people endure a crisis and become more bitter and withdrawn from life and others as a result. I have seen people endure a crisis and emerge scarred but grateful and ready to devote their lives to the service of others. What's the essential difference?

The answer I have for you is so simple and obvious you may be tempted to dismiss it. Don't. It is essential, a key to happiness. Try to hear it as if for the first time: A crisis such as your illness or accident becomes an opportunity *by your choice,* because *you say so.* The curse of your circumstance can be transformed into a blessing by the sheer power of your perception of it. How you choose to *label* the events in your life will determine your happiness, your peace, your success, and, in this case, your healing.

Labeling follows your perception, or what you choose to focus on when you look at anything. As it is for the weather reporter, it's completely up to you whether the day is partially cloudy or partially sunny. As it is for the child, it's your decision whether the glass is half empty or half full. As it is for the prisoner, the glance through the window bars can reveal mud or stars. Certainly it is not always possible to change the circumstances that surround you. But it is *always* possible to change the way in which you view or evaluate these circumstances.

When you stand up (so to speak) and make the choice for opportunity instead of anguish in your situation, you stand up against powerful forces with loud voices. With that choice you momentarily silence those voices from your parents, from your education, from your own feelings bellowing things like "This is bad, and tragic, and a punishment, and it will mean the beginning of the end for you and everyone, so you'd better confess, or panic, or take these pills fast, or whatever . . ." In that split second, you are changing history, you are distinguishing yourself as more than simply the product of your "training," as stronger than your passing feelings. You are in that moment a magician, an artist, a healer, a creator. You are transforming yourself.

When I suggest that you turn crisis into opportunity by making the decision to do so, I am not suggesting that you start celebrating the prospect of danger and pain. Rather, I'm advocating a basic life-choice—an orientation to living that requires courage, determination, and a true sense of humor. I am asking that you choose to start viewing everything in your life, beginning with this health crisis, as a potential gift, a mystery to be explored, rather than a problem to be endured. Why?

Because that is what it can be!
Because it is much more fun—and profitable—to do so.
Because there is already too much pessimism, suffering,
    and seriousness around.
Because it is a positive choice that creates positive energy
    . . . and positive energy heals!
Because making your choices *conscious* increases the power
    and control you have over your own life.
Because I say so!

---

*How carefully was that word
   chosen!
The word that allows yes, the
   word that makes no possible.
The word that puts the free in
   freedom and takes the obligation
   out of love.
The word that throws a window
   open after the final door is
   closed.*

The word upon which all
adventure, all exhilaration, all
meaning, all honor depends.
The word that fires evolution's
motor of mud.
The word that molecules recite
before bonding.
The word that separates that
which is dead from that which
is living.
The word no mirror can turn
around.
In the beginning was the word
and the word was
CHOICE.

TOM ROBBINS,
Still Life with Woodpecker

The Lessons Are Everywhere

Let's pretend that life is a school. Not a competition, not a trial, not a punishment or a reward for anything. Just a school. Let's further pretend that each person you meet is a teacher in this school—some are bright and humorous, some are dull and boring, but everyone teaches you something. Now, then, let's imagine that every event that occurs is part of the curriculum; sometimes the course is called On Finding a Job, sometimes the course is called Advanced Grocery Shopping. And to bring the whole fantasy closer to home, let's call this course you're now taking Illness and Recuperation.

Like anything else, you'll get out of this course, this school, what you put into it. You'll also have the chance to decide whether to fight it or whether to use it for all it's worth. This could be one of the most fascinating and meaningful courses you've ever taken. It may also be one of the hardest. But then, nobody said it would be easy.

Once you decide to redefine your crisis as an opportunity, you open the door to receiving the benefits and to learning the lessons it has to teach you—and they will be many. *Everything* teaches, if you are ready and willing to learn.

Crisis, and your response to it, can teach you volumes about who you are and what stuff you're made of. When the ordinary routine of life is suddenly interrupted, when the usual solutions no longer work, you have your greatest opportunities to grow, to change, to love.

Crisis destroys illusions, it exposes lies, and it relentlessly throws you back upon your own resources—your inner strength, the strength of your love and will. As Dean reflected on his time of crisis, he told me, "I use these memories all the time. My operation and all that preceded it will always help me to keep things in perspective. Now when situations arise that are difficult to handle, I temporarily take a step back from them until I can remember what is *really* significant."

In closing one door, crisis often forces us to open another. Following a heart attack, Nick began to take long walks as part of an exercise program to strengthen his body. During these walks he discovered a new way of being and seeing in general. He began to notice things in nature that he had never seen before—colors, changing patterns of light. Nick also found that his senses became more acute, making everything he did a more vibrant experience.

The literal meaning of "crisis" is a juncture or turning point. If you recall for a moment other critical situations in your life—a marriage or family problem, an issue at work—you can probably pinpoint how they motivated you to change, to move in a new direction. Each one taught you something. Each one generated new questions, with new choices to be made. Many seeming tragedies have actually yielded blessings. Many losses have led to future gains.

---

*T*urning points are the cauldron of our lives, the steps of our birthings, our self-formings.

STANLEY KELEMAN,
Living Your Dying

Jess Lair, whose books have inspired millions of people, found his life's vocation as a writer and teacher following a major crisis.

A heart attack at thirty-five led him to question and reevaluate the direction his life was taking. In his most famous book, *I Ain't Much Baby, but I'm All I've Got,* he writes: "As I lay on that cart, stripped of everything, I thought deep and clear for the first time in my life. I realized my whole life was screwed up. I realized I was doing a whole bunch of things I didn't believe in. I found myself saying, 'I'm never again going to do anything I don't deeply believe in.' "

Jess and his wife made a big decision. They sold their fancy house, sports car, even the business. Jess went back to school and earned a degree in psychology. He took a job on the faculty of the University of Montana at Bozeman and went on to write the books that have earned him worldwide appreciation. For Jess Lair, the crisis became the opportunity to learn to live again in a brand-new way.

When I broke my leg skiing, I got the chance to be alone for long hours and to face head-on my growing dissatisfaction with life. This was an uncomfortable gift to receive, but a necessary one. I know that over and over again I have used such situations, especially accidents and illnesses, as opportunities to stop, to look, to listen.

HOW TO USE YOUR OPPORTUNITY

Let's assume that you have in fact decided to answer the door when opportunity knocked. Let's assume you've chosen to redefine your crisis, to use it for all it's worth. Okay. Now what? The next questions may be, "Just how do I amuse this new guest? What do I *do* with the opportunity that has just walked in?"

Have you ever been entertained by a nervous or compulsive host—one who thinks that enjoyment is about filling up every spare minute with something to do, someplace to go? Does it not make you realize all the more that the most gracious host is the one who is relaxed and not trying to prove herself to you? Who cares for her own needs, so you never have to feel as if you're imposing? If things don't work out perfectly or the weather doesn't suit the plans, she doesn't apologize for things that are out of her control. She adapts with a smile.

Think of your good host as you prepare to turn your crisis into opportunity. I recommend the gentle approach, one that includes self-acceptance and self-forgiveness, as the most advantageous way to practice the fine art of recuperation. Such an attitude allows you to take advantage of the gifts that illness and crisis have to offer without adding any additional problems. You don't need any more stress than you've already got.

Walk the Gentle Path

Healing from illness or surgery is a lot like climbing a mountain. You reach one crest, thinking you're close to the top, only to find yourself facing another one. It can be a slow journey. And there are paths to the summit and back down again that are easier than others—paths that are gentler, a little shorter, more direct.

I learned about the gentle path only by fighting my illness, blaming myself, and following other paths that became dead-ends, trying to be "brave and strong" or "a good patient." When these didn't work, I explored another way and began sharing it.

Jim, at age forty, was a busy counselor and an aggressive business consultant. Balancing a family life with continuing his education and developing his career kept him working constantly. When medical tests revealed a possible obstruction in his colon, we talked about his concerns. He described his approach to life as that of being trapped inside an igloo. He imagined himself with a tiny ice-pick hacking at the walls of this self-made prison, wearing himself out but unable to stop. Life was equated with struggle, hard work. If he didn't keep hacking away—and that included an aggressive approach to "curing" his condition—he believed he would never get out.

"Suppose you just light a little fire inside this igloo of yourself," I suggested, "and sit quietly while you watch the ice melt?" I could see that he was confused, unable to entertain that it could be that easy. "Let your caring for yourself be the guiding principle," I offered. "You've already spent too much energy trying to muscle your way through." His face transformed. Touched with remorse for how rigid and demanding he had been toward himself, the tears in his eyes assured me that something had penetrated the ice. Putting his hand gently over his heart, he cried softly. He was melting.

Forgive Yourself, Accept Yourself

This gentle path to which I directed Jim is found by walking in self-acceptance and forgiveness, moment to moment, day after day. Over the years, each time I encountered a health crisis I observed how readily my fear, anger, or pain turned into self-blame or self-hatred. (The man or woman who wakes up from heart surgery and has to confront the fact that dietary habits of a lifetime have been a major contributor to his or her disease may be consumed with the same grief and guilt; it's a common response.) It took me quite a while to identify these self-defeating programs in my head, these internal messages of "You're bad!" or "You have no one to blame but yourself!" Often they were quite subtle. These thought patterns were undermining my health, and I grew to recognize what a price I was paying for them. And while I knew I couldn't silence them completely, I found that I could use them as triggers to remember something else.

That "something else" was the voice of compassion and forgiveness and self-acceptance—the voice of my inner healer or guardian. We all have one, even if we've muffled his or her voice for most of our lives. "Sure," mine said to me, "you've made some unconscious or uninformed decisions over the years. You've taken some calculated risks that didn't pay off. You've missed and ignored lots of warning signals, and even pushed yourself to the edge of the cliff before you admitted the truth about where your steps were leading. So? You are a human being, in process. You make mistakes. You do the best you can with what you have and know at the time. You can forgive yourself." Now here was a program I could live with.

It is often helpful to at some point examine the steps that led to one's crisis situation as a means of avoiding such unconscious moves in the future. But it is definitely not helpful to dwell upon past failings and chastise yourself for them. Because this is the reality now: You've got it (the crisis or illness), so what are you going to do about it? You've got it, so how are you going to live it from this point on? These questions keep us moving ahead in the direction of self-acceptance, self-forgiveness. These are the questions that support a gentle and complete recovery.

Take a moment now to select a phrase, an image, or even one word that signifies self-acceptance and forgiveness to you. I am moved each time I remember that "we do the best we can with what we've got." That phrase allows me to relax the rigid judgment I hold over myself. It softens my heart in a way that orients me toward forgiveness.

As time goes on I witness more and more that forgiveness is not some romantic or religious notion. Rather, it is a disciplined decision to *live in the present instead of allowing oneself to be dragged down by the past.* It is a practice that requires attention and caring to accomplish. Gradually, with time, it becomes a way of life.

Trust the Process

The more you can stay focused in the present, the more available you are to the miracles that are found only there. As awareness grows, so does respect for the profound wisdom of the body. You may come to appreciate how much the body wants to align itself with the order, the balance, the basic healthiness of life. You come to understand that the odds in favor of healing are overwhelmingly in your favor.

I found that to promote healing I essentially had to get out of my own way, to relax the fighting and worry and blame and concern for past mistakes that kept me in a state of resistance to healing; I had to keep the environment, inside and out, as safe and nourishing as possible; I had to remember that my mental, emotional, and spiritual concerns were every bit as important as my physical ones; I had to focus attention on what was going on here and now. In other words, I had to *trust the process.*

As hard as it may be to believe right now, you have physical and spiritual resources you are not even aware of that are going to be available to you as you need them: adaptability, creativity, courage, even humor. You have an inner strength that has rarely been touched, let alone tested. You are a creature of unlimited possibilities; a miracle; a magnificent human being.

---

*As soon as you trust yourself you will
know how to live.*

GOETHE

Pause for a moment, take a deep breath, and relax your hold on "doing" anything different. Recall now that the life in which you participate, the life that throbs in all your cells, is the same life force that has endured and been passed on since the beginning of time. Feel your connection to that primal life-stream. Realize your connection to the sun and the stars. Remember your connection to the plants and animals. Experience your connection with human life, past and present and future. Breathe it. Let go into it. Honor it.

Nature, time, God, and your own body-knowledge are all on your side in this healing process. Trust that. Allow this innate wisdom to do what it does best. This is the gentle path.

THE GIFTS OF ILLNESS

Jill wrote of her relationship with her father following his heart attack:

> During his stay in the hospital, I saw that Father was dramatically changing. He quit smoking without a thought. Six weeks later, after his triple bypass, changes on the emotional level were apparent. I saw clearly in him the quiet yet undefeatable warrior. The quiet part then began to give way to more overt expression—anger, pain, fear, love, caring, and joy. The power and directness of his emotion left me in awe, and I joyfully received all of it. This longed-for expression began to bridge a gap that had existed between us for years, rebuilding the bond that we had had when I was much, much younger. I felt "seen" by him in ways I had never felt before. This was an important step in accepting and celebrating myself as who I am!

Sometimes the side effects of our illnesses and accidents are profoundly beneficial to ourselves and others. The most awful things often have a way of working themselves "unto good," usually in ways that could never have been appreciated beforehand. This doesn't mean that we should court disaster. Prevention is always preferable to cure. But when the die is cast, and without denying the pain, we can turn crisis into opportunity by looking for the gifts. Think of what gifts your health crisis may be offering you at this time. Don't be concerned if you have not been able to "receive them" or "open them" yet. Just being aware of the possibilities is enough for now.

Following are a few of the gifts that others have found during their recuperation. Perhaps you've noticed some of the same.

- **Self-awareness.** This process of getting to know yourself—how you think, what it is you are really feeling, how body and mind are connected, what you need or want in any moment to further your recuperation, why you do the things you do—can deepen your friendship with yourself based on the simple appreciation of who you are.
- **What's essential.** The stripping-away process that crisis brings on can open your eyes to what's needed and what's superfluous in your life, your possessions, your relationships. Learning what you can get along without can serve as a back door to deeper self-understanding.
- **Gratitude.** The simple pleasures of breathing and seeing, moving and speaking, for simply being alive, overflows into everything and can, with intention, become a way of life.
- **Bigger perspective.** Like standing out under the stars, the perspective that illness can create may both humble you and amuse you. Anything that allows us to take ourselves less seriously is a great treasure.
- **Reassessment of life values.** Also known as the reorienting of priorities. It is here that you address the deeper questions that we all face. It is here that you start to plan for your future.

This kind of soul-searching is hard work sometimes. But the rewards it offers in terms of improving the quality of your life make it well worth the time and effort. Just suppose (and the possibility is very real) that you not only successfully recover from this health crisis but that you also manage to secure a deep peace of mind, a sense of satisfaction and happiness, and that you learn your lessons so well that you never again have to repeat them. Now, that would be a *gift!*

May you have many more.

NOT A QUICK FIX!

If nothing else, my illnesses have taught me this major life lesson: *There is no such thing as a quick fix.*

The choice to define and use your crisis as a gift instead of a burden doesn't make the pain go away. You're probably still going to hurt. You are still going to have bright days and dark days, up moments and lots of down moments. That's the nature of life and healing. What this choice does, however, is keep your energy channeled in life-affirming directions, and this creates a big difference in the healing potential of the body.

You don't just make this choice once and for all, either. Like making a good marriage or creating a good life, you will need to keep affirming your choice over and over every day . . . and many times a day. There will be countless reasons to give up, to fall back, to stay stuck in what's wrong. I know. It's easy to get discouraged.

So be tolerant of yourself when this happens. Recognize what you are doing. Quietly reaffirm your commitment to yourself, and keep looking ahead. Remember, this crisis is your opportunity—because you say so!

Think Yourself Well

You are much more than your mind.
You may think your mind is running
the show. But that is only because you
have trained your mind to think in this
way. You can also untrain and retrain
this tool of yours. Your mind is a tool
for you to use in any way you wish.

LOUISE HAY,
You Can Heal Your Life

Our thoughts, our words, the images we form in
our minds can enhance our recovery or discourage it. We can
literally think ourselves well. But, as Louise Hay suggests, tapping
this source of internal power will require some retraining of the
mind. Let's take a moment to reflect on this amazing tool, our
thinking mind. Appreciating more clearly how it can easily work
against us is paramount in the task of winning it to our side!
Consider the following stories:

Dorey was preparing for major surgery. She knew the prognosis for recovery. She knew the risks involved. As a student in a
holistic health class, she wanted to take full advantage of her
understanding of the connection of the mind and body in health.
So for several weeks before entering the hospital she engaged in
a program of talking to her body. She reminded herself over and
over again that she was strong and healthy. She told herself that
it was all right to relax and "let go" during the process, that she
would feel little pain, and that what she did feel she would not
resist. "You will have no unnecessary bleeding," she repeated to
herself, stroking her body gently as if assuring a friend that everything was going to be fine. "Your incision will close quickly and

cleanly. You will be full of health and life as you heal." After the surgery she continued her positive reprogramming. Every chance she got she directed her attention to her healing body, speaking words of encouragement, acceptance, relaxation.

Dorey left the hospital in record time! Talking to her at home, she was still congratulating her body for its remarkable recovery. Her doctors, she reported, were also amazed. Even the skeptics among them had found it hard to deny that something special had occurred in her case.

Paul, at age sixty-six, used a similar form of positive self-talk in recuperating from his heart attack:

> I walked myself back to health, and I got my mind muscles in shape at the same time. As I walked—back and forth, up and down the halls of my house—I kept repeating to myself, "I'm building a new heart. I'm building a new heart." And I believed it too. It would have been easy to get stuck in a different tape-loop, one that would have discouraged and probably killed me, like "I could have another heart attack any day," or something even worse. There are lots of men my age who think that way. But that kind of thinking is deadly. So I stayed with mine: "I'm building a new heart. . . ." I could even see in my mind's eye how the muscles were getting stronger, how the old cells were moving out and being replaced by new and healthy ones. I kept at it, and I believe I've done it. Within a year I was running a mile—and I haven't stopped yet. Now if I'm not walking or running, I'm swimming. This morning before dawn I saw three deer by the Platte River. I'm out every day no matter what the weather. How many people ever see one sunrise in a week? Not too many. But I don't miss one!

Writer and poet Rudyard Kipling knew the power of the word. "Words are the most potent drug that mankind uses," he wrote. I've watched people become radiantly happy right before my eyes when the right words were spoken to them. And I've also seen the opposite—breathlessness and fear, physical pain, loss of strength—all brought on by words that carried a negative message.

Following my accident in 1978, Dr. Robert Swearingen, an orthopedic surgeon, instructed me in how a broken bone heals and suggested that I visualize this process frequently. Bob had gained a reputation for his work with ski injuries, beginning with his training of ski-patrol members in how to help victims to relax. By using only healing imagery, he found that pain medication use could be significantly decreased and many fractures could actually be set.

Today, mind techniques are gaining in acceptance. Pain clinics throughout the United States, as well as many cancer self-help groups, use verbal reprogramming and mental visualization as keystones to their treatment plans. Let's look more closely at the role of the mind in wellness.

A MEETING OF THE MIND

Sam needed a whole battery of tests during his stay in the hospital. "The hardest part," he admitted, "was waiting for results. When day after day all I heard was 'Nothing conclusive,' I really started to worry with a vengeance. 'They're not telling me everything,' I thought. So naturally I imagined the worst. The words pounded in my head: 'Serious . . . incurable . . . terminal . . .' I began to feel weaker and weaker. And I grew angry. I was a victim of my own thoughts. All my old insecurities rose up to meet me. All the happy, smiling faces of nurses and visitors only increased my fears."

Worry is like that—a vicious circle. Like having a scratched phonograph record in your head, the mind sticks on one phrase and repeats it ad nauseum: "I can't take it. I'm only getting worse. How will I ever get my work done? I hate myself for this." Over and over and over.

Worry-thinking invades the cells of the body insidiously. It causes a tightening of muscles. It impairs breathing. It sets off a whole variety of chemical changes in your system. You know the outcome of that, and it isn't pretty. When you are confined to bed or limited by your recuperation, you will get to see and feel how powerful the mind is in effecting changes in the body.

Your mind is not your enemy, but it often acts that way. Actually, it is more like a stubborn child filled with demands or a highly sophisticated, computerlike machine. Like a child, its need for security makes it reluctant to give up its expectations. Like a computer, it runs only as well as the programming it has received.

Most of what we think of as "mind" is really only one aspect of it, namely memory. And what else is memory but a selective record of the past? When threatened by a health crisis, we are more vulnerable to fearful impressions. So it is understandable that memory may present you with its file of all the possible things that can go wrong.

Curiously enough, even when you are safe, cared for, and well fed, your body will react to the mind's imagined threats almost as strongly as if they were real. Say, for instance, you hear a loud crash in the night and think that someone is breaking into your house. The fact that it is only your cat makes no difference to your body. Heart rate and breathing change. So do blood pressure and hormone secretion. It's no wonder we often assume that mind and memory are not only running the show but in fact are the sole determiners of who we are.

There is another understanding about mind that may be helpful to you now as you heal. Put simply, your mind is actually split into two discrete modes of learning and remembering and processing information. One mode, localized essentially in the left hemisphere of the brain, is predominantly verbal, logical, sequential in its approach to things. This "mind" or "brain" is stimulated and programmed by words. It is with this "brain" that most of our conscious learning takes place. Most of us were educated verbally, logically.

The other side of the mind, in the right hemisphere, seems to have a very different outlook on life. It deals with pictures more than words. It is the artist, the musician, the nonlinear thinker. This is the brain that is impressed with images. This is the "mind" that is the gateway to the unconscious, that communicates only through symbols, dreams, and intuitions. Healing imagery "speaks" to this mind.

If you are to gain the support of both "minds" in your healing, you will want to address them in the language they each understand. Affirmative verbal messages and positive imagery or visualizations will work together to bring more of the mind under your conscious control.

Dr. O. Carl Simonton, radiologist and coauthor of *Getting Well Again* who has worked with cancer patients for many years, writes, "The difference between the patient who regains his health and one who does not is in part a matter of attitude toward the disease and belief that he could somehow influence it." Simonton has helped hundreds of people change their thinking about their condition by instructing them in simple techniques for relaxing the anxiety of the mind and focusing their mental imagery on pictures of health and wholeness. He has given them ways of rescuing themselves from themselves.

SIX DIFFERENT WAYS TO RESCUE OURSELVES

When Peter Pan was teaching the Darling children to fly, he had only to remind them to think lovely, wonderful thoughts, and up they'd go. And while some contend that it's that easy to turn your mind around, I'm not convinced. When programming of a lifetime has told us we can't fly or heal or even affect the condition of the body or emotions, it will take more than one pleasant reflection about ice cream or Christmas to get us off the ground.

On the other hand, little of value was ever attained without some energy and attention. So if you are willing to work with your mind, you will discover that it can be a great friend, a very powerful ally, and a creator of miracles.

The following six methods for mind-changing are not uniquely my own. In fact, most of them are age-old in their origins. In ancient Egypt, followers of the philosopher Hermes Trismegistres practiced the control of mental images as a way of affecting the physical universe as well as their emotional and physical health. And in the sixteenth century, the Swiss alchemist and physician Paracelsus believed that "the power of the imagination is a great factor in medicine. It may produce diseases in man and it may cure them."

Rescue Remedy 1: Conscious Worry

Just relax! Just stop worrying, okay?

If only it were that easy. In fact, *trying* not to worry, knowing that worrying is a wasted and even harmful activity, can tend to make you more tense than you were and can increase your worrying further. Now instead of simply worrying, you are worrying about worrying besides.

It gets pretty crazy, doesn't it?

The rescue remedy? *Allow worry to be okay.* The Japanese Zen master Shunryu Roshi, instructing his students in the calming of the mind, uses this analogy: "To give your sheep or cow a large, spacious meadow is the way to control him." In the same way, we can control our worries more by letting them come and go without trying to confine them.

Worries can also be tricked away. One approach is to worry consciously, vigorously. In previous steps we discussed how embracing our tears and fears, simply watching them "dance," will take the terror from them. And the same applies to worry. By resisting worry with tension, we only feed it. When we intentionally "dance" or "fool around" with worry, or when we give it more space to run, we tend to break its deadly hold on us.

The key word used above is *intentionally*. Once you *decide* to use worry consciously, then *you*, not *it*, are in charge. And that's the difference between being a victim of life and an active participant in life.

For right now, go ahead and let yourself worry—with intention.

Worry break. Start with a three-minute worry break. Instead of letting your tension build up against you, give it more room to move, but for a short time. My friend Ruth calls this the "poor pitiful Pearl" technique. As a child, she and her sister Marsha created Pearl as an imaginary friend who represented the most pathetic person they knew. Whenever they felt disappointed about something, they would "put on Pearl" and begin to moan, complain, whine about their problems or worries in their most exaggerated style. Before long they'd be laughing at each other's antics, relieving some of their tension.

I frequently play with my worrying mind by extending my immediate worry to its most dire conclusion. Try this if you want: Tell a friend what you're doing, and have him or her listen and join you in worrying. Or just talk to the wall, a picture, a mental image of whomever you feel like blaming for your fate. Spare no whining! Do it with energy. Pound on your bed with your fists if you wish. Kick your feet. Hit a pillow. Build your worries bigger and worse than anyone else's. Repeat your worry list over and over, out loud if possible. When the three minutes are up, stop. *Stop.* Promise yourself that you will put off your worrying until your next worry session. Now, turn your attention to something—anything—else.

Talk about it. As we've mentioned previously, lots of our worries are irrational. Indeed, you can be relieved by simply asking the right questions of the right people. When we keep our concerns hidden, they tend to grow out of proportion quickly. Enlisting the support of a trusted friend to be with you as you have a straight talk with your doctor, your employer, or your insurance agent is a valuable way to go about getting the information you need but may be afraid to talk about. Embarrassment is natural. But it can be deadly if it keeps you thinking and believing the worst.

Use experienced support. Talk to other people who have undergone a situation similar to your own. When Harriet was in the hospital for a mastectomy, her fears were enormous. "Then a vivacious young nurse visited me one day, and I was shocked to learn that she too had had this operation." Harriet spoke clearly and affirmatively as she reflected upon her experience. "I trusted her more than I trusted my doctor or my family members. I asked her everything, and she spared nothing. It was the first time I felt that I had been understood, and it changed everything. So many people increase their worries and fears by keeping them secret. There are support groups of all kinds, and if you don't know how to get in touch with them, just start asking. Nobody needs to go through such things alone."

Harriet's advice is sound. But it may not always be possible to find a willing ear. And during these alone times, when the worrying mind is wound up tight, you may find that the anxiety starts to leave you breathless. This is when you will need to apply your own emergency first aid—primarily breathing—for letting off the steam of worry and stress.

Rescue Remedy 2: Breathe and Visualize

Combine your imagination with your breathing and you will be utilizing one of the most valuable healing technologies possible. Try this one right now as I describe it to you. Let yourself breathe a bit more intentionally. A little more oxygen added to your system has a way of naturally relieving stress. Inhale and expand the abdomen as if it were a balloon. As you do so, imagine that you are inhaling only the purest, finest, richest molecules of air in your environment. The air now becomes your medicine.

Once it is inside your lungs, direct it all over your body, especially to the areas that need the most healing. It might help to "see" the air as sparkling particles of energy or a colored cloud moving through your body. Imagine filling all the empty space, the spaces between and inside all your cells with this healing air. Then release the air, allowing your belly to relax. As the air leaves your nose or mouth, imagine that it carries away your worries, your pain, your illness. You might even "see" the breath as being a different color or texture as you exhale it. Continue breathing in this way for three or four minutes. Then resume your normal breathing.

Rescue Remedy 3: Positive Memory Evocation

Memory has a powerful ability to depress you or to lift your spirits. Actors use it all the time to bring on tears by remembering a time of great personal pain, or to inspire enthusiasm and smiles by recalling an especially happy moment. This rescue remedy involves directing your memory to a particular time when you felt good about yourself, strong, energized, or serene.

Remember a time in your life when you showed tenderness. Who were you with? What happened exactly?

Take a few minutes to recall this incident. Try to re-create it in as many details as possible as if you were giving the information to a journalist who was going to write about it, or as if you were a film director advising your cinematographer how to shoot it. Close your eyes for a moment or two and "see" it taking place again.

What you are doing in this exercise is simply changing the movies in your mind from worrisome ones to health-inspiring ones. Do you remember a time when you felt awe? How about ecstasy? Joy? Compassion? The more proficient you become in re-creating these uplifting scenes, the more control you take of your thoughts. You come to appreciate that you *are* the director of that show that goes on between your ears.

Rescue Remedy 4: Mental Imagery

Most people do some form of mental visualization every day. Describe to a friend how you drive from your house to the nearest post office, and you are probably following the route visually in your head. Or think about the house you grew up in as a child. Recall your bedroom. Chances are you can "see" it in your mind's eye with a little effort. Visualizing is what makes listening to a story or following a radio drama so much fun. When applied to your health and healing, it becomes much more.

The method of imagery that radiologist O. Carl Simonton teaches to his patients combines relaxation with active visualization. It begins with stress-reduction exercises. Next, patients picture their immune system working vigorously, the way it is supposed to work. They are instructed to create mental scenarios of armies of healthy white cells armed with weapons that wound the cancer cells. Swarming over their weakened victims, the healthy white cells carry off the malignant cells and then flush them out of the body. To conclude each session, the patient visualizes his or her body fully well. Simonton's approach works to counteract the helplessness that many cancer patients experience. It gives them something to do that not only disciplines worry, but actually supports the body in healing itself.

Kay had a lump in her breast that required surgery. When I asked her how she was "seeing" it in her mind, she described a "black mass, with tentaclelike arms. And it's cold, and hard, and ugly. Evil." She went on: "I think of it all the time and imagine that it may be growing. A few minutes of this and I'm filled with fear."

So Kay learned a simple imaging-flip exercise, a method of rethinking and visualizing a healing process and a healing outcome. She started by drawing a picture of a healthy, clear breast. She chose yellow and gold colors and wide, circular strokes. Then she made a few more pictures, just like the first one. She placed copies of the picture in places where she would see it frequently— on the table beside her bed, on the door of her bathroom medicine chest. Then it was suggested that she compose a healing phrase, something positive to replace the broken record of worry that she was using now. She chose a simple one: "I am healthy and whole. I am healthy and whole." She now had two tools: one to occupy her inner image-maker (right brain); the other to occupy her inner message-maker (left brain). She was ready to go to work.

It was recommended that she take a few minutes several times a day to do nothing else but look at her picture, breathe deeply, and repeat her phrase. Each time she happened to glance at the picture casually, she paused for a moment to let it sink in. Whenever she became aware that her mind was stuck in her worry rut, she would acknowledge it without condemnation but immediately move on to repeating her healing phrase instead. She continued this process for two weeks.

When she next saw her doctor, he examined the lump and, in amazement, reported that it simply seemed to dissolve under his fingertips. He told Kay that he was truly baffled by the phenomenon. No surgery was necessary.

Perhaps it was only coincidence. Perhaps not. Certainly this approach will not necessarily rid anybody of tumors or disease. Many factors at work in each case determine the outcome. But I am positively convinced that with the mind on the side of healing, the body tends to follow closely behind.

This understanding has prompted many enlightened doctors to prepare their patients to deal with the discomfort and anxiety that may accompany surgery by using self-hypnosis or mental visualization. Patients who have open-heart surgery, for instance, are being instructed in relaxation techniques to help them accommodate the breathing tube that is temporarily inserted into their throats following the operation. Similar techniques for controlling pain and aiding in natural childbirth have been around for a long time. At the very least, working with calming imagery will enhance your relaxation. At best, the possibilities for other healing benefits are practically limitless.

To design a simple, positive healing visualization for yourself right now, follow these steps:

1. Start by recalling a time in your life when you were "all together," healthy and happy, even if that was for only a brief period. This could include a childhood experience, a vacation, or an athletic event in which you took part.

2. Focus in on one moment, one image of yourself that reflects this healthiest, most vital you. In my case, I see myself running early in the morning along a street in Toronto. I had just recently started jogging, and I felt great doing it.

3. Be sure this image includes your whole body, not merely a leg or your head. See your whole self working, moving in harmony.

4. Now make this image specific. The more details you can clearly "see" or designate, the better. Where are you? What are you wearing? Note colors, light, time of day, objects in your surroundings. Remember how good you felt, what you were thinking about—everything. In my visualization I am wearing my favorite, shiny green running shorts. My hair is long and tied up in a bright-yellow scarf. My arms are tanned. I am looking forward to the day.

5. Add to or subtract details from the picture until it works for you—that is, when you can almost feel yourself whole and healthy again. At that point you may notice a smile crossing your face, or sense a bit of enthusiasm or pride returning. These are good signs that your picture is working.

Don't rush the image-making process. This activity may take several sessions to accomplish. Allow enough time to work on it until you are satisfied that you have just what you want. Allow the *process* to be as rewarding as the product.

If you find it difficult to visualize, no need to give up.

Instead, *verbally* describe to yourself what your picture would be—for instance, "I am running down the tree-shaded street near my home in . . . My body is firm and trim. . . . I smile and breathe easily."

Feeling resistant to this process because your final goal seems too unrealistic at this time? Why not change the picture so that it represents *one small step* toward reaching the goal. For instance, say your goal is to ride your bicycle again. Start this process by forming the mental picture of yourself sitting on the edge of your bed, stretching your legs in a repeated pattern to gain flexibility and strength. When you find that you *are* stronger, then you may advance into forming a positive mental picture of your next step.

6. Reinforce this positive healing picture in as many ways as you can. You may start by using it when you realize that you are dwelling on negative thoughts. Practice it at other specified times as well, like first thing in the morning, each time the phone rings, or at every TV commercial.

   Write out the words HEALING IMAGE on a big sign and post it where you are likely to see it often.

   Do you have a photograph of yourself taken during one of your "peak" periods? Get it out and keep it around. Look at it. Comb magazines for shots of healthy people. Clip those and put them up. See yourself in the pictures.

7. Whenever you determine to use your healing image, start by relaxing. Close your eyes and take at least three to five slow, full breaths. Allow your whole body to "melt," to surrender into your bed or chair. Then formulate the image or describe the scene. Stay with it for about one minute . . . longer, if you desire. Then open your eyes.

More assistance in developing your skills in visualization, as well as other healing visualization exercises, can be found in appendix J.

Rescue Remedy 5: Positive Affirmations

You can increase the healing potential of your positive image by using positive self-talk along with it, or *positive affirmations*.

An affirmation is a verbal description of a desired condition. When used repeatedly and in many different ways, affirmations get programmed into the mind just the way those destructive messages of incompetence or fear got reinforced in your earlier years.

Those who study the technology of affirmations advise certain guidelines in working with them:

- Use the present tense.

  I am . . .
  I see myself . . .
  I feel . . .

- Simply describe the positive outcome you *expect*.

  I am growing in energy and strength.
  I enjoy riding my bicycle with ease and grace.

- Avoid tentative or negative words like "might," "maybe," "hope," "will be," "don't," "not," "never."

Here are some healing affirmations to choose from or to use in composing your own:

With every breath I grow in energy and strength.
My mind, my body, and my soul are all working together
    to create healing and peace.
I am at peace. I love and accept all of life.
I release the old and welcome the new. Health and
    happiness are mine.

Combining your positive healing affirmation with a positive mental visualization will reinforce the desired outcome.

Every time you think you are not happy, say, "I am happy." Say it strongly to yourself, even if your feelings are contradictory. Remember, it is your self-image and not you. Just as fast as a fish can move in water, you can instantly change to a happy, balanced attitude.

TARTHANG TULKU RINPOCHE,
The Self Image

Rescue Remedy 6: *Mind Watching*

This most challenging and most rewarding remedy has been saved for last. Just how well do you know your own mind? Have you ever simply traced the progression from one thought to another? Have you ever wondered about *how* you think? How you come to a decision? How do you arrive at a creative insight? Do you think in color? Do you think in pictures or in words?

Learning to be a mind watcher requires diligent practice in detaching yourself from the content of your thoughts so that you get to understand that your thoughts are not in charge, even though they may seem to be. A mind watcher can laugh at himself or herself, can refuse to be hypnotized by thoughts that normally would have incited fear and pain, can learn to substitute more health-inspiring pictures for gloomy ones.

In Buddhist practice, this technique of mind watching, a form of meditation, is known as vipassana. To do it, begin by sitting still. Then close your eyes and just watch your thoughts. As you watch, remain dispassionate about whatever shows up on the screen of your imagination. Let your breathing be smooth and regular. Do not assign judgment to anything the mind does, or any place the mind goes. Merely report what is going on, label it, and let it pass on. The labels are broad: a "desire," a "worry," a "question," a "judgment," a "childhood memory," and so on.

Watching the mind in this way tends to slow everything down. It rests you. It encourages compassionate distance from pain-inspiring reverie—those tragic movies that play over and over in your head. Watching gets you in touch with a you that is bigger and deeper than mind, a you that is running the whole show of your life, a you that wants to *use* the mind rather than be *used by* it.

Ways to mind watch. Mind watching can be done as a routine or ritual at a particular time of day, for ten, twenty, or even more minutes at a time. Another way is to stop yourself often in the midst of whatever you are doing and to say to yourself, "Hello, are you there?" In the moment of awareness that follows, you step back inside of yourself, noting your thoughts and where they were taking you.

Use cues to trigger attention to your thoughts. For instance, every time you take the cap off your medicine bottle, hear the phone ring, or glance at a clock, let that remind you to check in with yourself, to watch your mind again. "Hello, are you there?"

I have used a favorite picture or sign placed in a location where I'm sure to notice it from time to time as my cue. I observe it, take a deep breath, bring my attention to what I have been thinking, note it, and then let it pass on.

If this form of meditation and awareness practice is appealing to you, refer to appendix K.

A WORD OF WARNING

Changing your mental attitude is a key component to recuperation. The attention paid in this chapter to thinking, visualization, and self-talk is necessary because, by and large, most adults are still being "run" by beliefs learned or adopted as young children. Even though the beliefs may be unrealistic or completely fantastic and no longer serve us, they may still remain strong.

One of the side effects of each of the rescue remedies suggested here will be a clearer perception of some of these core beliefs, those fundamental building blocks on which we have constructed our thinking patterns. Unfortunately, we will often discover that we have been building on some very shaky foundation. One of the most common beliefs, "I'm never good enough," seems to be at the root of most of the illness and unhappiness in people's lives.

Realizing this has prompted many different approaches to belief-system renewal, from metaphysics to cognitive therapy. Louise Hay's book, *You Can Heal Your Life,* is excellent in this regard. For those who need a more standard, psychological approach, the works of Dr. Albert Ellis and the popular best-seller *Feeling Good* by Dr. David D. Burns are recommended. (More references to these and others can be found in the Resource Guide at the back of the book.)

The fine art of recuperation will take you as deeply as you want to go in understanding yourself. The process may end, but the end tends to lead to a whole new beginning in itself. Nevertheless, there are those well-meaning friends and peppy self-help books (one hopes not this one) that will instruct you to "look on the bright side of things," to "be brave," to keep a stiff upper lip and not to complain. Otherwise helpful counsel may indirectly encourage you to deny what you are really feeling and may discourage emotional expression.

Stop everything!

We know that positive thinking and visualizing are invaluable to healing, since everything you think and believe has an impact on your body. Keeping a clear mental picture of yourself getting stronger, feeling better, resuming your normal activities, and accomplishing your life goals is undeniably an energizing, hope-building, and relaxing process.

But *positive thinking should never be used as a denial of your real feelings.*

Feelings need expression, at least through conscious acknowledgment. Feelings are instructive. Denying them is foolish, tension producing, and even dangerous.

What is essential here is to maintain a *balance.* It is possible, and positively therapeutic, to both express your emotions (acknowledging your fear, your pain, your confusion) and in the next moment to focus your mind on the positive outcome you desire. In fact, these two movements can be used to complement each other. Every negative feeling or distress emotion can be a cue to remind you of your positive intention. The cue becomes a built-in feedback mechanism to help you achieve the balance that allows you the optimal conditions for healing—namely, honesty and hopefulness.

Open to the Spirit

> The most beautiful experience we can
> have is the mysterious. It is the funda-
> mental emotion which stands at the
> cradle of true art and true science;
> whoever does not know it and can no
> longer wonder, no longer marvel, is
> as good as dead, and his eyes are
> dimmed.
>
> ALBERT EINSTEIN

In times of personal crisis, people with a strong religious faith and those with none at all will ask themselves the same questions: "What's really important?" "What is the nature of life and death?" "What endures? What dies?" Frequently they touch upon some "thing" that is bigger, more vital, than anything they have encountered before. Perhaps because of the presence of intense fear, or sometimes because of the supreme effort it takes to survive, we become more vulnerable. And this vulnerability seems in a way to open us to that which is ineffable—the mysterious, the real—be it God, or truth, or life.

Many people in recuperation tell stories of personal trans-formation—a reorientation of values and priorities, the forgive-ness of lifelong grudges, the dawning of spiritual insights and awakenings, even a few minor miracles. Such breakdowns as ill-ness and accident seem to create openings into the realm of spirit, the domain of being and meaning, in ways that few other life experiences can.

Judith, once diagnosed with breast cancer, wrote this many years later:

That diagnosis was a catalyst for change in my life in so many ways. It forced me to realign my priorities about how I wanted to spend my time, specifically my career time. My traditional career as a librarian has been put aside as I prepare to work in ways to help others of my generation cope with the challenges of this new age.

The diagnosis has also propelled me in my personal search for wisdom and the connection with the divine within. For me this has not been any one or two peak experiences of shattering illumination in which I suddenly became one with God, but rather a long, winding road on which I occasionally caught glimpses of what I felt to be some power, something larger and grander than myself. This struggle to connect with a universal core, this knowing that I am part of something more meaningful than the day-to-day struggles of life, continues to be a dominant theme in my life today.

The lasting changes brought about by illness are seldom immediately dramatic. More likely they are quiet, subtle transformations, the effects of which are witnessed only slowly, over time.

Health crisis may not be the best door to a larger potential, but it is one that almost all of us will eventually face, and its multidimensional possibilities should not be wasted.

RICHARD MOSS, *How Shall I Live?*

OPEN DOORS

Recuperation offers each of us a series of openings, like doors that are slightly ajar. Behind each door is a possibility for further exploration and for deeper appreciation of some aspect of life. The signs on the doors are as varied as the people who approach them. Many people have explored those marked GRATITUDE; SILENCE AND SOLITUDE; FEARLESSNESS AND FORGIVENESS; and RECONCILIATION WITH DEATH. Let's examine each of these.

Gratitude

During Fred's recovery period, his wife, Pam, would drive him out into the country to watch the sunset. "I especially loved looking at the cornfields," he commented. "They were such a solid reminder of life. I was so happy to be alive I just wanted to hug that corn or roll in the dirt . . . anything to express the overwhelming joy I felt at this marvelous aliveness."

To this day I remember with exhilaration how I too felt when, upon returning from India, still weak with illness, I sat down to my first home-cooked meal in nine months.

I made the determination there and then that I would never again take life for granted. I would never again eat or drink or breathe or walk without *knowing* what I was doing, without being grateful for it. I was determined to make gratitude my way of life.

Sad to say, my appreciation of each simple thing faded rather quickly as my strength returned and work piled up. It happens to everyone—like the wealthy man who was washed overboard from his yacht a long distance from land. As he realized the slim possibility of ever making it to shore he prayed: "Oh God, if I ever get there I promise to give my entire fortune to the church." With renewed energy he swam until he had covered three quarters of the distance, with strength to spare. Seeing now that he was considerably closer to the goal, he continued his prayer: "Thank you, God, for your help, and don't forget that when I make it, I'm donating half of what I own to the church." By the time he dragged his exhausted body onto land, the gift had diminished to 5 percent.

But even though my gratitude waned and the memory of those painful months in India have faded mercifully, *something* remains. Practicing gratitude serves as a potent medicine for times of discouragement or panic or fear. It demands that you look around at what is right at hand. It forces you back into the here and now, requiring that you keep your feet on the ground, that you keep things simple. I know that my own illnesses have moved me a step closer toward that realm of spirit characterized by a more expanded appreciation of life—toward a life of gratitude—and that yours can too. Here is what I wrote about this process in my journal:

> I want to live my life here and now, not waiting until this is over so I can start to enjoy. I want to savor everything—the sound of the

water dripping from my roof, the brightness of the sun, the cold I feel in my feet and fingers, the taste of the banana, the struggle, the conflict, the tender touch. Everything. I refuse to die without having lived. I see that living only happens in the present. I will open all my senses to this appreciation, this now, this gift of God.

Silence and Solitude

In *Summing Up,* W. Somerset Maugham describes an enforced confinement to bed in a sanitarium because of tuberculosis:

> For the next two years I led an invalid life. I had a grand time. I discovered for the first time in my life how very delightful it is to lie in bed. It is astonishing how varied life can be when you stay in bed all day and how much you find to do. I delighted in the privacy of my room with the immense windows open to the starry winter night. It gave me a delicious sense of security, aloofness, and freedom. The silence was enchanting. Infinite space seemed to enter it, and my spirit, alone with the stars, seemed capable of any adventure. My imagination was never more nimble; it was like a barque under press of sail scudding before the breeze. The monotonous day, whose only excitement was the books I read and my reflections, passed with inconceivable rapidity. I left my bed with a pang.

The introduction to silence and aloneness that Maugham describes is for many people an opening into self-knowledge, a spirit opening of tremendous magnitude and depth. How rare it is for most of us to have unstructured time: time to listen within, time to pray. Although we hunger for the nourishment that solitude and silence can provide, how often do we allow ourselves the luxury? Even if we take off to hike the mountains or to camp in the wilderness, the survival activities necessary during such trips keep us busy enough to avoid such steps into infinity.

As you make friends with silence and solitude, you make friends with yourself. You come to know the terror, the wonder, the paradox of this life that you have been absorbed in for however many years. For myself, I came to understand that this "I" (who I *think* I am) is mostly a series of conversations that go on in my head. In these conversations I describe myself, I judge myself, I counsel myself. The deeper I listen, the more I hear that these conversations are replays of messages from parents, teachers, the media. Finding a voice that speaks for itself in the midst of these many conflicting voices, finding a voice that resonates with truth, rather than one that simply echoes the voices of others—this has become the work of my life.

Following a major car accident, nurse-educator Susanna Davis felt the impulse to explore her inner depths. In an article from *The Heart of the Healer* she writes: "I took myself away to a friend's farm and proceeded to explore 'listening' to a language that was rushing out of my heart whenever I would relax and be still." Sharing this approach with the clients in her practice is invaluable: "At any given crisis point in living, whether it is an acute or debilitating illness or mental or emotional disturbances, each person has the key to his or her own starting point in the healing process." And this key finding occurs in the spaciousness provided by silence and solitude.

The journey into self can be a risky process. Few road signs point the way. Continually thrown back upon your own sensitivity to truth, your own discernment of which direction the spirit is guiding you requires ruthless honesty and a great deal of compassion. You are always a beginner, a pioneer on this frontier.

The journey into self through silence and aloneness is never easier for one than for another. But the fortunate ones are those who remember that uncertainty is not an enemy; that complete, logical understanding of who we are is not possible. The spirit opening that silence and solitude afford is an opening into a type of "knowing" that isn't taught in school. Silence and aloneness offer an opening into knowing the true self.

Fearlessness and Forgiveness

In his book *Shambhala—The Sacred Path of the Warrior,* the Tibetan Buddhist master Chogyam Trungpa Rinpoche writes about the subject of fearlessness. Fearlessness does not mean without fears, but rather an attitude of heart and mind and a resolve of soul whereby one moves ahead *despite* one's fears. It is this characteristic, he says, that distinguishes the warrior, the fearless one, from the mediocre person who lives a life confined by fears.

When my friend Peggy wrote me to express her fear that she "didn't know how to be sick" or how to help herself get better, she hoped I'd be able to tell her something to help her. "You need to know that no one goes through loss and pain in a clean, clear way," I wrote in reply. My letter to her continued:

> From reading or hearing stories, you sometimes get the idea that other people know how to grow through their sickness and grief in a way that is eluding you. But that is generally not true. What you read or hear is usually smoothed out by the passage of time and the perspective created by some distance from the source of the pain. I have found that when you are right in the middle of your illness, very little is straight or clear. The path through is much more of a constant wiggle that leaves even the strongest of us feeling dizzy and confused at times. Stumbling, bumbling, fumbling, and grumbling—that's how most of us make our way. The important thing is to keep moving ahead anyway.

Trungpa further points out that the most primary fear that the warrior must face is the fear of his or her own self—just like the abiding belief that you are somehow not good enough, not worthy of life, no matter what you do.

If these attitudes of distrust and fear are present in all people all the time, then they are definitely spotlighted during times of illness and recuperation. And this can be dangerous when we need the focus to be on self-acceptance to further our healing. It seems that a big part of developing fearlessness occurs when we make the decision to forgive ourselves for being human, for not being perfect, for getting sick.

Healing is always about relaxation and expansion. Anything frightened or dead is closed, contracted, rigid. What is alive is moving, open, spacious, supple. Everything that encourages expansiveness within the body, the mind, or the emotions encourages healing. And that is precisely what forgiving yourself does. It relaxes, expands, and thereby heals you.

In their book *Patienthood,* Miriam Siegler and Humphrey Osmond write, "The central issue in convalescence is forgiveness. The rule seems to be that unless you can forgive yourself and others for your illness, you cannot recover."

To forgive means to refuse to hold onto the past; to release grievances, recrimination, blame; to reconcile. It includes the willingness to look beyond or beneath the surface appearances, the "acts" or "masks" of yourself and others, to connect with the place in which basic goodness resides at the heart of each being. To forgive is to appreciate your atonement (at-one-ment) with everything that is.

Forgiveness creates the peace of mind that shows up in the body as relaxation of judgment and rigidity. When that occurs, the body is freed up to heal itself. There is harmony. Dr. Gerald Jampolsky, who has worked for years with children and adults in life-threatening crises, holds this connection between self-forgiveness and harmony in the body as the major underlying principle of his practice.

Forgiveness is a choice, not a feeling, even though a sense of relief and letting go is often experienced. To practice forgiveness, you simply make the intention to do so. If you fall short of your goal time after time, day after day, continue making the intention. Patience is the key. Your willingness to forgive yourself and others is the monumental step. Renewed intention slowly and surely takes its effect.

Reconciliation with Death

Illness has a way of reminding you of death. When you feel strong, active, and healthy, you can distract yourself with work, with movement. You can "knock on wood." You can shake it off. When you are weak or inactive or alone in bed with little to do but think, it may hit you a lot harder.

Even a cold or some other relatively minor ailment is enough to trigger remembrance of mortality. For Donald, the trigger came from a more serious condition, but his reaction to it was surprising. Waiting for help to arrive after he crashed his car, he remembered:

> I felt as calm and at peace as I have ever thought possible. I said to myself, "I suppose I might die or I might live." I had no energy going either way, just a realization that it *would* go either way and that either way was okay with me. I really felt deeply unafraid. I did not will to live, nor will to die. By quietly just being, I consciously set aside my preferences. This was a real sense of relief. Not a letting go of anything or any specific result. I prefer to describe it as an opening . . . an opening to the profound mystery of life.

Many people like Donald discover that a close brush with death allows an "opening" of such magnitude that they never again fear dying. For others, myself included, confronting death has never yielded a permanent reconciliation. Rather I find that I must make my peace with death and my vulnerability and my mortality every day, moment to moment, over and over again throughout my life.

Illness *is* a death of sorts, like every other situation of loss in life. Every time I feel the sting of lost independence, of giving up my sense of control, of admitting that I don't know something or that I might be wrong, I practice "dying" a little. The practice of dying in this way is really a dynamic way of living. It is an attitude that keeps one always on the edge, a beginner. It demands that you constantly give up your position of being right. It keeps you respectfully humble.

The poets, saints, and sages have always said that life and death are not opposites. Rather, like the inhaling of air that fills the lungs and the expelling of air that empties them, life and death are complementary parts of one ongoing process. In fact, the word for "breath" and the word for "spirit" in many languages are one and the same. In English, we speak of "inspiration." This can mean both the taking in of air and the act of being filled with the spirit. The word *expiration* can mean both exhalation of breath or letting go of the spirit in death. In every breath something is dying in us and something is born.

"I know that life and death are a continuum," Fred said at the end of a long recuperation. "I know that being a human being is just a step along the way. I can't prove it, but it doesn't matter because I'm not trying to convince anybody else."

There is an old story that Plato, on his deathbed, was asked by a friend if he would summarize his great life's work, the Dialogues, *in one statement. Plato, coming out of a reverie, looked at his friend and said, "Practice dying."*

STANLEY KELEMAN,
Living Your Dying

Illness is for me an opening into a greater appreciation and respect for the life I have now. It has allowed me to grapple with the big questions of meaning, and in that very struggle I have come to know myself better, to contact a divine presence in my life, and to love myself more.

One thing that facing death has taught me is that the old saying "If you've got your health, you've got everything" is not completely true. Health is *not* everything. You can have health and still not be loving, learning, or happy, and you can be ill and yet open to these. Just think of all the great people handicapped by deafness, blindness, or paralysis who lived remarkably rich lives.

Of course health should be cultivated as a sacred trust. But the self-obsession that comes with trying to defend against illness or death is much more devastating to the human spirit than infection. If health were the number-one priority of life, people would be sorely pressed to risk anything in order to serve others.

Gratitude, silence and solitude, forgiveness and fearlessness, and the willingness to look death in eye have been "gifts of the spirit," but gifts that you must work to achieve. Even if that work amounts only to relaxing yourself enough to receive the gifts, you need to orient yourself in their direction. In my own life I often had to push myself a bit to move forward despite the pain, the fear, the inability to "feel" forgiving or grateful or resigned to death. I had to remember something that I couldn't always feel and definitely couldn't prove: that I was *good.* That healthiness was my natural state. That happiness was my inheritance.

Spiritual strength comes from being solidly rooted in this knowledge and appreciation of one's basic goodness. This is what it means to practice the fine art of recuperation. And this is the opportunity, the priceless gift that our health crisis has offered to us.

Take a moment now to think about your own self-discoveries, the inner revelations of this current period of your life. What "doors" have you approached? Which of them are you deliberately avoiding? Which have you opened? There is no need to force the process in any way. It is simply a good idea to stay aware of how you are moving through it.

HOW TO ACCESS THE SPIRIT WITHIN

You may now be asking yourself how you might access this knowledge of your basic goodness and tap into the inherent wisdom of your body and mind in ways that are practical and instructive. You have probably heard, as I have, the counsel to simply *listen to yourself.* But many of us find that without a definite structure or ritual for doing this, the voices within get drowned out by the noise and activity without.

Throughout this book stress-reduction exercises and breathing techniques are used to quiet ourselves, smooth rough edges, draw ourselves back to center. They prepare the ground in which a deeper "listening within" may grow. Following are a number of approaches you are sure to find helpful in focusing your "inner ears" on the spirit within us all.

Let Your Dreams Speak to You

From ancient times, priests in Babylonia and Assyria called upon their dreams to reveal information necessary to the survival of the people. They used dreams to diagnose illness and often sent the patient to a temple to sleep and dream. The healing dreams that occurred during this "incubation" period were thought to be significant to the understanding and curing of the diseased condition. The ancient Greeks did the same. Their healing temples contained special sleeping rooms to which patients retired at night. Here as they sleep they might be visited by priests dressed as gods who touched their diseased parts and spoke to them to stimulate dreams. In the morning, the person would begin to carry out the instructions given in the dreams.

If you do not already record your dreams and inquire of them, use this recuperation to begin that valuable practice. Since you will be doing a lot more sleeping these days, why not make the most of your time of incubation?

Recognize that what is speaking to you in dreams is your own unconscious mind couched in symbols that may be difficult to understand at first. The more you work with your dreams—writing them down, thinking about them, asking for them—the more they begin to come clear. One night as I fell asleep I asked for specific guidance about my health. I was awakened by the voice in the dream speaking loudly: "You are taking too many mineral supplements." I followed my own advice and felt better.

Listening to the symbols and persons in our dreams and interpreting them as parts of ourselves is a way of promoting the kind of questioning that leads to self-understanding. Say, for instance, you have a dream of playing Monopoly with your friend Larry. Ask yourself what you associate with Monopoly. (Perhaps it means financial growth, taking risks, opportunities.) Now ask yourself what you associate with your friend Larry. If you see him as a hard-working person your dream may be reinforcing for you the connection between hard work and financial abundance. (Except of course, if Larry is losing the game badly, in which case the opposite might be true.)

Either way, you need not worry about having a professional analyst to help in this interpretation game. All you need is the willingness to inquire more deeply of yourself. Occasionally, if we are lucky and aware, a dream may communicate an undeniable connection with that which is larger than ourselves: a sense of divine communion or the realization of our unity with all life.

Inner Dialogues: Let Wisdom Write

Writing quickly, without initially rereading and without censoring (as much as that is ever possible) is an effective tool to accessing knowledge and guidance from the spirit within. One technique especially useful in times of illness is the dialogue-writing process, in which you have a "conversation" with a symptom or ailing body-part, and you write down this conversation as it develops. The results can be surprising. One woman who had an ongoing problem with headaches discovered in such a dialogue the rigid and demanding messages she was giving herself. Her headache suggested that she address it with more gentleness, acceptance, and love. When she began to "speak" to this part of her body more caringly, her chronic condition began to improve.

Say, for instance, your problem is a weakened heart. Begin by imagining your heart, and then start to have a conversation with it that you record as you go along. First write out what you say, then write out what you imagine your heart saying. It might go something like this:

Me: Hello, heart. You've given me quite a scare lately.

Heart: You're not kidding! That was no fun for me, either.

Me: I'm worried about you now. I keep wondering if you are strong enough to support me again, the way you used to be.

Heart: That's going to depend a lot upon the way you treat me.

Me: What do you mean?

Heart: You need to make sure that you take me into account as you eat and work—you know what I mean. . . .

As the dialogue continues and lengthens, you may find that you are telling deeper and more significant truths to yourself— things that you have always known, things that you have been unwilling to admit, occasionally startling things. Don't expect that everything you need to know will be revealed in your first dialogue. Your "inner wisdom" is like a new acquaintance. It holds back a bit at first to determine if it can trust you to honor it, to be patient with it, and to listen to its suggestions. In much the same way that dreams become instructive when you attend to them seriously, the inner guidance that reveals itself through your writing will grow stronger and clearer over time.

Meet the Doctor Within

Personifying inner wisdom is one way to access it. This exercise for contacting your inner doctor, or healer, adapts and combines various techniques. It is simple enough for even the most inexperienced mind explorer. I call the inner guide and healer in this exercise your "house doctor."

The house doctor is yourself, of course. What this exercise attempts to do is to set the conditions so that you may contact this knowledgeable, sensitive, but less conscious part of yourself again.

The house doctor knows you intimately and has only your best interests at heart. He or she is waiting to be called upon to answer your questions with a firm, authoritative voice, a voice that speaks the truth and quiets superficial chatter and worry. You'll recognize this voice when you "hear" it. A sense of rightness, an inner relaxation will accompany it.

To make an appointment, read over these instructions before

you begin the experience. Better yet, record them and play the tape to yourself, or else have a friend read them to you.

Preparation. Lie on your back, close your eyes, and become aware of your body as it is now on your bed. Feel the parts that are in contact with the mattress and the parts that are exposed. Scan your entire body from toe to head and sensitize yourself to the space you occupy.

Now begin to surrender yourself to the bed. Let go completely in every muscle, in every cell, letting the bed support you. Feel yourself sink into the bed. Sink down through the bed into the floor; down under the floor through the earth; all the way through the earth and out into limitless space. Enjoy the free-floating sensation of resting in space.

The meeting. As you float, notice that a beam of light shines from your body, and like a headlight it illuminates the space in front of you. Have this light lead you to a station in space—a platform, a planet, a "place." Land here. Wait.

Look around you and above you and realize that you are alone. Let this awareness penetrate each cell. Notice that the beam of light is still shining from your body. Follow the beam back to its source deep inside yourself. Stay there at this source point, looking, listening, feeling whatever is there.

Find yourself standing in front of a huge mirror and look at yourself. Notice that your face is smiling and soft—very appealing. Your eyes are gentle and compassionate. Everything in your reflection is loving and trusting and peaceful.

This is your inner guide, your wisdom source, your truest self. This is your house doctor.

The conversation. Now speak to yourself. Ask all the questions that are on your mind. Ask for advice, for encouragement, for energy. Be specific. Share everything that you already know to be true about the questions you are asking. Express your doubts and fears as well.

Now, be silent . . . and listen.

Drop your expectations of how the answers will come. Just be aware. "Watch" as images appear or scenes are enacted or words flash on the mirror before you. There is no telling precisely what form your communication will take. Stay very quiet and alert, and listen some more. Resolve to remember what you have learned.

The completion. Whenever you are ready, thank your doctor for meeting with you. Ask if she or he will meet with you again. Set up an appointment for the near future. Acknowledge the information and especially the love with which it was shared.

In your imagination create a gift to give your doctor and hand it to him or her. Watch carefully to note if your gift is accepted and appreciated.

Decide to leave this place now, and feel yourself once again back in touch with your body. Wiggle your fingers and toes. Stretch. Take a few energizing breaths, and open your eyes.

You may argue that you only fabricated this whole scenario. What of it? If you learn something, remember something, or reconnect with your wisdom source, you are the richer for it. Be grateful.

Anchor Yourself: Use Prayer

Prayer is whatever you understand it to be. Whether you call it conversing with God, or appreciating your connection with the infinite, or allowing yourself to be moved by universal life energy— whatever, it's up to you. When I open myself to a higher power, a greater wisdom, I find that my access to my own inner wisdom opens even more. The boundaries between who I am and what the *that* out there is, tend to dissolve. It's a paradox. The more I lose myself, the more I find. The more I let go of, the more I seem to have and know. In my own journal, I recorded this thought:

> There is a providence, a divine providence, that is tangible at times. When complete helplessness is embraced as a friend, rather than resisted as a sign of weakness, a power greater than myself has moved in and moved through my life. I have felt my connection to a universal life energy, something that bonds me to all other life. The normal boundaries of personality and flesh that keep me separate have dissolved or blurred on these occasions. I become attuned to a realm of existence that is characterized by limitless energy, by grace, by ease and profound humor. The laughter of God is what runs it all. What else can I say? Life is a dance, a play, a great and gentle flowering. Amen.

For me, to pray is to sit quietly in the face of the mysterious, and to wonder.

Move Back into Life

You have a rendezvous with life.
ERIC BUTTERWORTH,
UNITY MINISTER

Helene had just left the hospital, ten days after her back surgery. Now, as her husband helped her up the stairs and over the threshold of their home, she found herself crying. But her tears were not those of relief and gratitude, as you might expect. Rather, Helene was crying, she told me, because she was stepping back into life as she had known it. Life, complete with its problems, its minor frustrations, its push-and-pull relationships!

In the hospital I was safe. I was special. I was cared for day and night. As much as I hated to be an invalid, I loved being taken care of and so well. But now I'm home and I'm afraid. Confused. There's no nurse to call for. I have to ask my husband for help—constantly. I hate to see him so anxious about me. I hate all the extra work he has to do. I am terribly sensitive to everything he says to me, since I take it all personally. I continually wonder if I'm doing too much or not enough. But the worst part is I have to pick up the old worries I left behind when I went to the hospital. They didn't just disappear. Sometimes I just wish I could be back in the hospital again. Is that awful?

I told her I didn't think it was awful at all. In fact, I thought her observations were remarkably precise and honest.

We all long to be safe, cared for, made to feel special. And that's what people try to give us when we're sick. When it's time to move back into life again, it's natural to experience some longing for the safe place we have left. It's just another face of grief.

For many people the retreat and rest that illness offers are a welcome relief. Getting well may temporarily involve the loss of status, of care, or of safety. But this too shall pass!

As you prepare to move out of bed or to call this recuperation period to an end, appreciate as Helene did the subtleties of grief. Expect the ebb and flow of your energy as well as your emotions. It's all part of the process.

THE REINTEGRATION PROCESS

Your recuperation is a process to be lived; it is not a deadline to be met. And like any process, there may be numerous false endings. People who have gone through the grief of a loss find that even long after acceptance or resolution, they still experience "aftershocks"—surprising, short-term relapses. Don't be upset or think that you are losing ground if this happens for you. Your process will be over only when it's over, and it may continue for a long time yet. While you're going through something like this, it's rarely possible to see the whole picture. "Patience furthers," advises the Chinese sage. So, with this in mind, take that first step.

Don't Overdo It

Your tendency may be to want to jump back, immediately, into life as you left it. Don't.

Besides, you can't! Life will never be the same for you after this experience. If you try to make it just as it was, you'll be liable to find yourself right back in bed again, sooner than you imagine.

Some externals of your life may need changing—your diet, your exercise patterns, your manner of driving your car, your six meetings every week. Even if nothing "outside" changes, you need to *change the way you view your life circumstances*. It's time for less seriousness, less intensity, less compulsiveness. It's time to see problems as opportunities. So, please, as you climb out of bed, do it slowly.

Take it easy. Give yourself lots of extra sleeping time. Say no to at least three demands every week. Keep the upper hand for yourself in dividing up your time; that is, resolve that *you* will control your schedule, instead of letting the schedule control you.

Recognize the stress that you have just been through, and if at all possible avoid adding other stress-producing events at this time. A move to a new location, a significant job change, a major responsibility—these can perhaps be postponed until you have had more of a chance to stabilize your health.

Walk through life where previously you ran. Eat with attention and care. Take the time to breathe, to notice things. Feel textures, smell aromas, enjoy colors. Go slowly. Your friends and colleagues will understand. In fact, they probably expect it. As each new day dawns, be grateful for increased strength and health. Look at each aspect of your life and ask: "Does this need doing now, by me?" Learn to delegate. Keep your priorities very clear, the first of which is by now self-evident: your total healing.

One should not carry moderation to extremes.
ARTHUR KOESTLER, BRITISH WRITER

Don't Underdo It

Bodies in motion tend to stay in motion; bodies at rest tend to lie there. Inertia breeds more inertia. If you lie around long enough you'll never be asked to dance again, and this tendency toward invalidism must often be resisted with vigor. It's understandable. You may worry that you will strain yourself and bring on another accident, heart attack, or serious illness. And that's a serious consideration.

Three remedies deal with this fear: First, trust your body's natural inclination to healing; second, trust your doctor's recommendations; and third, speak to others who have been through similar circumstances; they will be your strongest sources of ongoing inspiration. Work these three together, and you'll have a winning combination.

If your doctor or therapist prescribes exercise—*do it!* Don't stop to think about it. Resistance to moving is natural in your recovery stage. Keep at it. Even if you do your exercise in waltz time, listen to and obey your doctor.

Every day give yourself a new task to accomplish on your own. Slowly but surely start to reclaim control of your life. Start making dates to meet in a relaxed setting with friends you haven't seen during the course of your illness; see those who served and visited you while you were bedridden.

The decisions you make at this stage are crucial to the rest of your life, as you engage in setting up an entirely new series of life programs. Realize how important that is. Keep asking yourself: "Is this activity serving life and health?" If the answer is yes, do it. If the answer is no, forget it. Stay very aware of any tendency to use your illness as a way to excuse yourself from situations you would rather avoid. If you don't want to do something, then don't do it, but quit rationalizing that it is because of your illness. Tell the truth to yourself and to everyone else. Review all the payoffs that this experience has given you, and start asking for these things more directly.

Reach Out to Someone Else

Confined in a full-body cast, Marge was miserable, full of pain and feelings of helplessness. One day her hospital bed was wheeled into the room of a frightened young woman who had been involved in a serious car accident that had left her with multiple fractures. Marge's work simply amounted to "being there" for the young patient, encouraging her to talk, to cry, to do whatever she needed. In the midst of her own pain, Marge was able to serve someone else. And this service became a way of healing herself. She began to feel useful. She treasured the chance to put aside her own drama for even a short time in order to touch, with understanding, the life of another.

Reach out to those people closest to home. How can you serve those who are serving you, or living in your home, or sharing the same hospital room? Ask them. Tell them that you want to help. Discuss together how this is possible. Confined to bed with my broken leg, I filled many hours with a sense of purpose by doing little things for the people who cared for me—sewing on buttons, mending hems, stitching cuffs. It wasn't much, but it was a task, and accomplishing it had great rewards for me.

The telephone is a powerful way of reaching out. Talk to other shut-ins. You've become something of an expert in recuperation, so why not share yourself?

In *Reconciliations,* Dr. Theodore Isaac Rubin recounts the story of Mary, a young patient in a mental hospital. Mary was so detached from reality that she never spoke and rarely moved. All therapeutic attempts to reach her had failed.

One day Dr. Rubin introduced Mary to Rose, an older woman who shared the same ward. The doctor indicated that Rose could use some help and suggested that to Mary. At first Mary simply sat next to her new friend. After a few days she took Rose by the hand and began leading her around the ward. Within a short time Mary was feeding her. She was beginning to really care about Rose.

Slowly, Mary began awakening to her own life. She started speaking. Her improvement was steady. Eventually she was able to be released from the hospital.

In her service to Rose, Mary had stumbled upon the very key that unlocked the door to herself.

Few people can fail to generate a self-healing process when they become genuinely involved in healing others. . . . Selflessness is the greatest weapon in integrating and aiding the self.

THEODORE ISAAC RUBIN,
Reconciliations

The art of genuine service requires vulnerability. One way to do this is to express your *own* feelings—your fear, your pain, as well as your acceptance, your own ways of coping, your favorite jokes. This opens a door to communication and allows the other person to admit what is happening without fear of judgment.

If you can write, send notes to others in need. Write an article for your church newsletter or send a letter to a local newspaper, encouraging others who are in a situation similar to your own. Many permanently handicapped people have written books detailing their own stories of overcoming seemingly impossible odds to live a happy life. How about writing your own book?

These suggestions are not meant to impose an additional

burden on yourself. In the early stages of recovery, your first priority is to *strengthen and heal yourself.* Trust that you'll know when and if it's time to reach out to others. But remember that all you give to others is given to yourself as well, since you are connected in an essential way to everyone who lives. So if you feel you are ready to reach out to others and heal yourself by doing it, start today.

Write Your Story

As we've discussed earlier, many people find tremendous value in writing during a process of grieving and recuperating. If you can hold a pen or pencil, try writing out a description of the health crisis you have been living through. Do not censor anything you write. Daily, if possible, chronicle the new challenges and questions that arise as you recover. Look back over your writing every few days or so as a way of charting your progress and encouraging yourself to continue with self-exploration and self-development. Write out your personal goals, short term as well as long term. And refer back to them often.

Use the following questions to summarize what you have learned and are learning now. Refer to them in the future to keep moving toward optimal self-awareness and health. Write your answers in your notebook or journal or simply ponder them—alone or with a spouse, close friend, or supportive person.

- What have been the payoffs of this experience? (That is, what have you allowed yourself, as well as what have you excused yourself from?)
- What elements in your lifestyle in the six months or so preceeding this breakdown may have contributed to this condition?
- Express your thoughts and feelings about the following issues as you view them now: economic security, a comfortable life, education, relationships, family, job, religious values, death, crisis.
- What are you grateful for in your life?
- What are you appreciating more as a result of this condition?
- Who and what have you allowed yourself to forgive?

- What advice and help would you offer to your best friend if he or she were to have an accident or illness like yours?
- Is there any way you can serve others as a result of this experience?
- What has been the hardest part of this whole experience for you?
- What has been the greatest gift of this entire process?
- How will you use the knowledge gained in this challenge?
- What will you *do* within the next three days to support your life enhancement?

Complete Unfinished Business

If a room is packed full of furniture, it leaves little space for dancing. The same is true about the past clutter we accumulate in our lives. Lots of unfinished business restricts newness, spontaneity, and joy. Creating spaciousness allows for abundance and miracles.

As you move back into life, try to clean up loose ends, and complete what you left undone in the way of projects. But don't forget that there may be other unfinished business concerning relationships that could use a little attention now too. Perhaps there are people to thank and acknowledge for their support during this time. Perhaps there are people to forgive. Call them. Write to them.

You may be much more aware now of your own mortality. Let the presence of death as friend and teacher motivate you to live each day with gratitude and attention, healing the past all along the way.

❦

Stay Well

> The simple truth is, happy people
> generally don't get sick. One's atti-
> tude toward oneself is the single most
> important factor in healing or staying
> well. Those who are at peace with
> themselves and their immediate sur-
> roundings have far fewer serious ill-
> nesses than those who are not.
>
> BERNIE SIEGEL,
> *Love, Medicine and Miracles*

In the *Wellness Workbook,* which I coauthored with
John Travis, we strove to define what was then the newly emerging
concept of wellness:

> Wellness is a choice—a decision you make to move toward optimal
> health. Wellness is a way of life—a lifestyle you design to achieve
> your highest potential for well-being. Wellness is a process—a de-
> veloping awareness that there is no end point, but that health and
> happiness are possible in each moment, here and now. Wellness is
> the efficient channeling of energy—energy received from the envi-
> ronment, transformed within you, and sent on to affect the world
> outside. Wellness is the integration of body, mind, and spirit—the
> appreciation that everything you do, and think, and feel, and believe
> has an impact on your state of health. Wellness is the loving accep-
> tance of yourself.

If this definition sounds familiar, that's because it is practically
synonymous with the fine art of recuperation as I have expressed
it throughout *this* book. The work of staying well is no different
than what you've been doing throughout this healing process,

except that now you have more energy and strength to help you to carry this work forward. Use what you have learned in this fine art of recuperation as the basis on which to build a lifestyle that supports health. Because now you know that a well person

- allows and expresses emotions as vital and positive life-signs;
- listens to and respects the needs of the body;
- cultivates a balanced relationship with time and lives as fully as possible in the present moment;
- practices self-responsibility and active participation in life;
- recognizes his or her connections to all other human beings and serves and honors them accordingly;
- is able to redefine crisis as opportunity, knowing that perception of events in one's life is what determines happiness;
- uses the mind in ways that support creativity and a positive outlook;
- lives in remembrance of spiritual values.

IT'S ALL ABOUT ENERGY

When Einstein stunned the world with the little equation $E = mc^2$, he was simply telling us that what we think of as solid matter is really just energy in motion.

Practically speaking, this means that your body, too, is a moving field of energy, as is the sunlight streaming in your window, the chair you're sitting on, the water you're drinking, and the blood that's circulating now in your right foot. Stretching the concept beyond the physical, you can see that even nonsubstantial realities like thought or emotions are energy phenomena, since they arise within the energy system of your body-mind and definitely affect its operation.

The more clearly you can appreciate the energy dynamic in your body, the better able you will be to design and maintain a lifestyle that supports you in staying well.

A Primer about Energy and Well-Being

The body is an energy system: a generator, a transformer, and a distributor. Your body absorbs energy in the forms of oxygen, food, and sensory stimulation like light, warmth, and touch (the input). It then works the input over, changing these energy forms into blood or bones or electrochemical signals to the brain. Finally, it sends some of this transformed energy out as movement, conversation, and work (external output), while the rest is used for inner work—repair, replacement, or rebalancing (internal output).

The quality and quantity of your output, both internal and external, is a direct function of the quality and quantity of the input. The efficiency of the whole system, moreover, depends upon the good working order of the many parts and the ability of energy to flow unobstructed throughout. (This is beginning to sound a little like an analogy to antifreeze or motor oil, which is actually not such a bad parallel.)

So, what does this mean for you now as you set out to live well again?

For starters, it gives you a simple, consistent model to explain the dynamic behind every aspect of healthy life. Like why you need to rest—which is *to conserve or build your energy;* why you'll want to eat healthy foods and breathe clean air—*to supply you with the best raw materials around that can then be converted into the most powerful energy;* why you're better off sharing your concerns and feelings—*to avoid stockpiling energy necessary for other things, like healing;* why exercise is so important—*because it is a means of directing energy throughout the body;* and why overall relaxation is so vital—*because it keeps all your energy channels open.*

The wellness viewpoint is that all illness, weakness, disease—whether physical, mental, or emotional—is a result of *energy lack, energy blockage or contamination,* or *energy loss* in some form or another. Health, on the other hand, is the result of increased and high-quality energy input, efficient energy channeling and balancing, and the elimination, as much as possible, of energy dissipators or drains. So if you're asking yourself why you feel more tired after being with certain people or eating certain kinds of foods, your knowledge of energy transformation should answer the question for you. Anything or anybody that saps your energy naturally slows down and diminishes the energy you need for ongoing health.

What energizes you may be slightly different from what energizes me, because we are each unique. But in general, it is safe to say that energy is accumulated by resting, eating good food, breathing clean air, breathing more fully, receiving natural sunlight, looking at beautiful surroundings, reading uplifting books, listening to lovely music, communing with a higher power or nature, strengthening your self-esteem and sense of control of your life, and best of all by allowing yourself to receive honest support, touch, and caring from other human beings.

What loosens up blocked or repressed energy includes intelligent exercise, deep breathing, massage or loving touch, sex (sometimes), forgiveness of yourself and others, crying or sighing and other forms of natural emotional release, writing or speaking your questions, fears, and concerns to compassionate others (or at least to yourself), laughing, laughing, laughing, and being honest rather than exhausting yourself with being nice or trying to keep up a brave front.

What prevents unnecessary energy loss is more rest, moderating worry in general and especially worry concerning conditions that cannot be changed, focusing on the here and now instead of living ahead of schedule, asking clearly and directly for what you want and need, being gentle and compassionate toward yourself in all ways, easing off of guilt and regret in any form, associating with people who make you feel good and not encouraging those who drag you down, and avoiding addictive habits like smoking, drinking alcohol, or using nonprescribed drugs.

You are a kind of engineer, coordinating the environment so that energy can flow optimally. But you have the added responsibility of operating in areas where medicine can't touch—inside your thoughts, your soul. All of you—mind, body, and spirit—needs to participate to maximize your full potential for wellness. Your entire energy system needs to be nourished, stimulated, balanced, and nurtured if you are to live well now.

TWO CORNERSTONES OF WELL-BEING: RESPONSIBILITY AND INSPIRATION

In the Chinese symbol for the Tao (see next page), two opposites, black and white, are blended in such a way that a perfect circle is formed. This symbol represents the dynamic union of forces that keeps the world in motion: male and female, darkness and light, water and dry land, active and receptive modes of being.

When it comes to staying and being well, maintaining health and vital energy, two approaches must be balanced as we undertake the journey. On the one hand, we need the discipline, the structure, and the commitment to do what is necessary in order to

stay healthy. This is the arm of the process I refer to as self-responsibility. Then there is the other arm, the one that embraces rather than directs, which I call inspiration.

People create a discipline for their lives that moves them toward wellness because they are inspired to—either by themselves or some other person or thing. Similarly, people tend to keep inspiring themselves when they discover that discipline results in their feeling a whole lot better about themselves, when it produces the changes they seek. One balances the other; one feeds the other. Discipline without inspiration is cold, sometimes even cruel. Inspiration without discipline is simply ineffectual.

Take Responsibility for Your Life and Health

Taking responsibility for your life and health is to be an adult in the world. And simply being forty, sixty, or eighty years of age does not necessarily mean that we have attained adulthood. To be a grown-up in this regard means that we recognize that nobody else is going to do it for us—make us or keep us healthy—and that includes our spouses and especially our doctors and other health professionals. At some point we must stand up on our own and declare what it is we are striving for—namely, a long-term, high-quality life. When we acknowledge this, we structure our lives accordingly.

For some of us that means a change of diet. For others it means a change of environment or job. For many people the first step is most often the hardest. After that, the process tends to build momentum when we actually start feeling better.

Starting small, by setting realistic goals and realistic action-steps, is very important, especially at the beginning. For instance, if you need exercise, start by walking at least a few blocks a day and plan to increase the distance and speed over time.

Remember, self-responsibility doesn't exclude help from outside. In fact, quite the opposite is true. The responsible person draws help from all appropriate sources—books, people, classes, trips, or other experiences. So keep an open, ongoing relationship with sources of help, including your doctor. Talk to him or her about your continued health and well-being. Listen to and honor your doctor's advice. Discuss your own thoughts and feelings, and make informed decisions accordingly. If there are classes or support groups for people who have had illnesses similar to yours, participate in these groups. If no groups exist, why not start one for yourself and others? It doesn't have to be a formal one, either; your neighbor down the block who walks two miles a day may be all the support you need. Just having another person to work out with will go a long way in helping you keep to your schedule. Discipline may be a dirty word to some, but for me it means a form of honoring oneself.

Keep in mind that responsibility for and guilt or blame over something are very different. The former gives you power and control; the latter robs you of the same. So be diligent with yourself in accepting responsibility for your life and health. Refuse to take the easy road of giving up by doing nothing and then feeling guilty about it.

Every person, all the events in your life are there because you have drawn them there. What you choose to do with them is up to you.

RICHARD BACH, *Illusions*

I really don't know exactly how much we can control about our health and our lives. In some cases it is evident that our lifestyles set the stage for our accidents and illnesses; in other cases, there isn't a clue. But one thing I do know is that the people who *act as if* they have the majority voice in what occurs in their lives are the people who *create* opportunities for themselves all around.

One way to make this attitude tangible is to listen as you speak to yourself or others and to observe how often your language betrays lack of power and control. Listen for "victim-speak," that attempt to constantly blame life circumstances on other people or things. If you find yourself saying "I can't . . ." about anything, try substituting a phrase that more directly confirms your primary role in the creation of your reality. Use "I don't choose to . . ." or "I won't . . ." or "I don't know how . . ." and observe the difference that this word change makes.

Another specific means by which to practice self-responsibility is to take up or expand your study of yourself—physically and in every other way. For one person that might mean taking a nutrition course; for another, reading about some aspect of psychology or personal growth; for yet another, counseling or participation in a self-evaluation workshop or seminar program.

The more we learn about ourselves, the more confident we are in asserting our rights with the medical establishment—and every other establishment, for that matter. The more we learn about ourselves, the more we may be inspired with gratitude for who we are, what we know, and what we have been given.

Inspire Yourself to Wellness

There is a Sufi tale about a rug seller who walks through a town crying out the price of his wares. "Only one hundred gold pieces for this rug!" he proclaims. And indeed, his rugs are magnificent. A wise man, seeing the quality of the seller's goods, is amazed at the low price and so questions the rug dealer about it. "Why are you asking only one hundred gold pieces for this marvelous rug?" To which the rug seller responds questioningly: "Is there any number greater than one hundred?"

We limit ourselves by what we think is possible. If we think that one hundred is the highest number in the world, that will be all we can ever get. If we think that we are capable of only so much health, happiness, and satisfaction in our lives, that will be essentially all that we are ever going to find. If we are convinced that there is one and only one way to solve something, we will never discover anything. What we find is, by and large, a function of what we go looking for.

On his ninetieth birthday, George Burns quipped: "I only hope the second half of my life is as good as the first has been." In 1996, when he turns 100, Burns is scheduled to play the London Palladium for two weeks. "You know, they don't usually keep you there for two weeks," he said in an interview. "You're lucky if you get to play a day."

This is the attitude of the *lover of life.* It is one of the strongest guarantees we have for ongoing health, for happiness, and often for longevity. The way to stay well in the present is to look to the future with wonder and joy.

People who have a sense of wonder about existence, who cultivate a joyous anticipation, who live in the realm of "What is possible?" as opposed to the realm of "This is inevitable" heal faster and more completely. And often they extend their lives, qualitatively and quantitatively, beyond what their doctors expect or statistics predict. These are the people who experience miracles, as Dr. Bernie Siegel has shown us. These are the people who are grateful for life as it is, even when it's tough.

This brings to mind Margaret and Sam. At eighty-four and eighty-two, respectively, they are among the most vibrant human beings I know. I have been moved to tears just listening to Sam's description of a sunset or a new rose that he has cultivated in his garden. He and Margaret are both still full of wonder about the beauty and mystery of life, and consequently they inspire the same in others who are around them. They are not afraid of making long-term goals. In fact, as active members of a national peace organization, they continue to take on increasingly greater commitments.

These healthy, "wonder"-full friends live in a state of "brand-new-ness." They are not solidified or crystallized in their concepts, their way of thinking, their traditions. Flexibility and the willingness to risk, to try something new—these are their outstanding characteristics. There is a childlikeness about these people. They will approach you with a question rather than a challenge when you say something they don't agree with or don't understand. People who cultivate wonder and well-being have learned by experience that *they* are the determiners of happiness, not the circumstances in which they find themselves. In each situation their approach is:

What can I learn here? What can I do to serve here? What's possible?

To be and stay healthy, we need inspiration. That was my motivation in writing this book—to inspire you with self-appreciation and to share the inspiring stories of others who have walked this road before you.

It isn't hard to find inspiration once you start looking for it. Inspiration to life and health is everywhere, and it is infectious. Once you catch it from yourself or someone else, you'll just naturally pass it on. There is always something to be grateful for. It may only be necessary to slow down long enough to notice.

It has always been clear to me that learning and loving were integral to the process of well-being. Eating whole-wheat bread or jogging a few miles a day is just not enough. Of course, it is important to eat well and to exercise, but it is *essential* to reclaim your own inner knowing, to accept yourself as you are, and to look to the future with joy.

What will it take to inspire yourself and stay inspired? For me the inspiration process has four steps. The labels come from my friend Ruth, who uses them in her counseling practice.

1. *Awareness.* You always start from where you are, looking with compassionate eyes at where you are not inspired in your life, as well as where and how you are inspired. Remember, as much as possible, the essential goodness that you are.
2. *Forgiveness.* This means being willing to let go of past failure and mistakes. Give yourself the opportunity and the time to grieve the fact that you haven't been and can't be perfect.
3. *Decision.* You make a choice to open your heart to the wonder of life. You *decide* to be inspired, even if you don't feel inspired.
4. *Action.* You move, speak, try, allow, consider, study, visit, call, read, listen to, risk—whatever it takes, day to day, to encourage your inspiration.

We are inspired when we open our eyes to what is all around us, starting with what is right under our noses. Nothing is too small. Nothing is too big. And it's never too late to start.

Don't hesitate to draw from many different sources to maintain your inspiration:

- Seek out healthy role models to keep yourself inspired to be healthy. Learn from a healthy role model how it is possible to keep going despite pain or adversity. The artist Goya, for instance, at eighty years of age and in near-blindness, drew the picture of a very old man and inscribed it "I am still learning." Healthy role models can serve as sounding boards for your discouragement. As they console you, they will also not let you forget your inner strength, your inner resources.

  Remember the people who inspire you, the Sams and Margarets in your life, and use them, even if they are physically unavailable to you now. An imaginary conversation with your role model can be every bit as effective as a real one. It's all a matter of listening inside your own heart a little more carefully.

- Find some heroes or heroines. Read a biography of a great person who overcame odds to make a contribution to humanity. Or of someone who got a late start and finished triumphantly—like Gandhi, who didn't really recognize his life's vocation until he was in his fifties; or the writer Cervantes, who was well into old age before he became a novelist; or Saint Teresa of Avila, who admitted that she didn't seriously approach her work until she was past forty. Post a picture of your new hero or heroine in a prominent place and remember their courage.

- Focus on the positive. Read magazines or newspapers looking for the *good news* and start a scrapbook of life-affirming events and people. Share the good news you discover with everyone you meet and speak with over the next few days or weeks.

- Cultivate appreciation for the arts. Listen to music that lifts your spirits. Watch movies or TV shows that provide hope and reinforcement of the power of the human soul. Treat yourself to a visit to an art museum, a date for a dance performance, or a symphony. Read yourself a poem each day, or pick up that classic novel you've always wanted to read.

- Set aside a space and time each day for silence and solitude, when you do whatever it is that feeds your mind or your passion, whether it is prayer, poetry, some hobby or craft, reading, writing that book you have dreamed of writing, or deliciously doing nothing.

- Take risks. Try new things and be enthusiastic about something, with no apologies to anyone else. (You may be interested to know that "enthusiasm" comes from the Greek *en-thousiasmos,* which means "the god within you.")

- Spend time with or simply observe children—they can help you remember what it means to live in wonder, to be inspired.
- Think big. Cultivate a belief in God or something larger than yourself! I know of no better way to be and stay inspired—and hence to be and stay well—than to work on behalf of some impossible task in a way that produces results. When you give yourself a big goal, you multiply your chances of living healthily into that future. So think big. Think of the condition of the whole planet, the needs of children everywhere, all the sick who are currently discouraged that they will not survive what you have just been through.
- Embrace all sides of life, as well as yourself. Recognize the potential for energy that is present everywhere—in the subways as well as in the parks. Accept your dark side as well as your light side, your discouragement as well as your joy, knowing that it is all just a different view of the face of life. Remember the story of the man with the wonderful horse, and hold off on your final judgment of things or yourself . . . indefinitely! Just take it easy. Take it as it comes.
- Live in gratitude. Take a few minutes each day to thank yourself for anything and everything you have done in supporting your own life and life in general. Remember to be grateful for everything and you will remain inspired and healthy, even with illness, until the day you die.

You might have done things differently if only you had known then what you know now. The past, however, cannot be changed. But the possibilities in the present and the openness to a more vibrant future . . . these are areas over which you do have some control. Perhaps what you have remembered in using this book will inspire you to let go of yesterday and to make choices now in favor of a healthy tomorrow.

❧

A Personal Healing Journal

If you are new to keeping a journal, bear the following in mind:

Know that there is no one right way to keep a journal. There is only your way. I used my own journal during times of recuperation to sketch in, to record my dreams, to write out new ideas I had on life, to try my hand at poetry, and to compose letters that I knew I would never send. You can use your journal for any or all of these purposes, or for whatever else comes to mind.

Be honest with yourself. Dare to admit to your journal what you are afraid to admit to someone else. Converse with yourself as if you were a most trusted friend. Address yourself by name if you care to: "Yes, Jerry, things are tough right now . . ."

Avoid self-editing and self-criticism. You will do yourself a big favor if you write quickly and avoid reading over your work until you feel it is complete. Since so much of our unhappiness is often the result of feeling inadequate, many people have the tendency to stop themselves from producing something out of fear that it will be unacceptable. However, you will be amazed at how easily and prolifically you can express yourself when you put the critic to rest for a while. Just do it!

Don't be limited by writing or speaking logically in only full sentences, or even in words. You may really enjoy challenging yourself with different modes of expression. If you usually write only narrative, try poetry for a change or draw with crayons for a few days. Try using a tape recorder, sing to yourself, or just make sounds that feel good or express your feelings.

Date all your work. This is a valuable way of charting your progress.

WHAT TO WRITE ABOUT

- *Tell the story of your illness or accident.* Start at the very beginning and record everything you know to be true about it. Do this again in a week, and observe if your outlook is different in the two stories.
- *Have a dialogue with your illness, a part of your body, or another part of your mind.* Give that part a voice and a name of its own. Ask it about the crisis you are now experiencing, why it is happening now, and what it has to teach you. Be courageously candid. Examples and further explanation on this method of dialoguing can be found in step 8 of this book, "Open to the Spirit."
- *Start a conversation* with a wise teacher, a spiritual leader, a famous doctor, or anyone else who you know can help you in your recuperation. Perhaps you want to talk to God or to the wisest, kindest heart specialist in the world. Begin by writing a letter to your confidant, giving the person a name. Communicate your deepest feelings, your needs, and your fears. Then, write a reply to yourself from your new friend or teacher. Give yourself advice. Love yourself. *Be* this other for a while, and have him or her share an inner knowledge with you. You may be very pleasantly surprised at how much you can learn.
- *Play with the past.* Look back over the scrapbook of your life. For example, recall the three most important decisions you have ever made, but suppose that in each case you had made another choice. What difference would that have made? Tell your life story now, incorporating these three new choices. Of course you have no way of knowing what would have happened, but the point is to make it all up for the sake of a good time and some insight.
- *Dream up the future.* Imagine that ten years from now you meet yourself on a park bench in Paris. The person you meet is magnificent: healthy, strong, gentle, compassionate, successful. Describe in detail what you are like. Have a conversation with yourself revealing how you managed to turn out so beautifully.
- *Make lists.* For example, as an aid to self-pity, make a list of all the things you can't do or be as a result of your current

situation. Don't be satisfied with simply listing the things you might normally do; also include items that you've thought of doing or always dreamed of doing or being. Or try this one: Imagine that it is three years from now and you are looking back on your recuperation. List all the ways you wish you had spent your time.

- *Go on a cruise.* Create a fantasy of the most pleasurable confinement you can imagine. Pretend you are the only passenger on a small cruise ship crossing the Pacific Ocean. The trip will take three weeks. You have a tiny stateroom and a lounge chair on the deck. Write about what you will do to spend your time. If you could have only one other person along, who would that be? Ask a visiting friend to share the fantasy with you for some additional ideas. Bon Voyage.
- *Write or compose poetry.* To create poetry is to capture with words a moment worth remembering, be it joyful or painful. Writing poetry is not difficult. I believe that poetry is poetry because the author says its poetry. You don't need to burden yourself by trying to make the lines rhyme, or by comparing your attempts with those of famous poets. Consider the following as jumping-off places from which to write your poem:

> Reflections. Make a running list of all the things you remember about your childhood home and some of the pleasant things you did there. ("I remember the clock in the hall that ticked louder than usual on the nights when I couldn't sleep." "I remember the smell of . . .") Your list becomes your poem. Enjoy it.
>
> Love. Look around your room and choose any object that catches your eye. Now create an explanation of why love is like that object. Do this several times. ("My love is like a TV set; it just sits there until I remember to turn it on.")
>
> If. Begin with the statement "If I had my life to live over again I would . . ."

There are many books about journaling to inspire you in your work. I recommend Tristine Rainer's *The New Diary: How to Use a Journal for Self-Guidance and Expanded Creativity* (Los Angeles: Jeremy P. Tarcher, 1978).

Prescriptions for Emotional Help

R_X 1: RECOGNIZE THAT YOU ARE NOT ALONE

Your normal life may have been turned upside down or inside out by this health crisis. The grief or panic that accompanies such a major upheaval may leave you feeling quite insecure or wondering if you are losing it or going crazy. But these reactions are normal.

The first prescription for riding the sometimes frightening or confusing emotional waves that accompany a health crisis is to recognize that you are not alone in what you are going through. Others have felt this way too, and often. And while this may not relieve your pain, it may help to relieve some of your anxiety about it. Truly, nobody else has ever experienced crisis in *exactly* the same way you have. Yet the reports of many recuperating people about what they felt, what they feared, and what surprised them are remarkably similar despite age differences or types of illness.

To encourage you to heartily grasp this idea that you are not alone, it will be helpful to simply read over the following list of common feelings and thoughts gathered from many recuperating people, myself included. As you read, check off those that you too identify with. Talk over any especially troubling feelings with a friend or your doctor.

Recuperating people report that you are more than likely to have these common reactions:

- Impatience, thinking that you're not healing fast enough.
- Strong and strange emotions, like depression, anger, sadness, fear—things that you haven't felt in years, or maybe ever.
- Increased emotional sensitivity, even rawness at times, taking everything personally—the weather, the news, the moods of family and care givers.

- Reluctance in asking for the help you really need because you don't want to burden others any more.
- The need to make lots of resolutions about the things you'll change if you get the chance, or else do differently or never do again. Bargain making with God, your family, yourself.
- Boredom beyond description.
- Near obsession with what's going on in your body, watching the movement of every gas bubble for fear it is another heart attack or the growth of something ugly.
- Rerunning all the low points of your life, especially your failures and all the rotten things you did to others.
- Discovery that your closest relationships are strained.
- Blame and even hatred for yourself for your illness or accident.
- Being haunted or obsessed by the worst moments of your accident or illness.
- Asking, "Why me?" over and over and over again.
- Feelings of violation, of having been stripped, exposed—cut open and ripped off.
- Feeling absolutely ecstatic, overwhelmed with gratitude and enthusiasm for life, just happy to be alive. And in the next moment, feeling desperate and sad, lonely and hopeless.
- Refraining from sharing your pain, feelings, and questions with others, even those who can help. Wanting to keep everything, or at least something, to yourself.
- Sensing that you are *out of control.* And not liking it!
- Wanting to be a good patient by being brave, not complaining.
- Being so confused and worried that you just wish you could turn off your mind.
- Liking the specialness, the caring, and the attention you receive from family, friends, and nursing staff when you are laid up.
- Being secretly glad that your illness or accident has given you an excuse to rest, or to not go someplace or do something.
- Deep remorse or guilt for how you neglected your health or for how you "set yourself up" for this accident or illness.
- Thinking about dying. Feeling scared. Wondering if your life has made any difference so far. Avoiding painful thoughts.
- Wanting to blame your spouse, your boss, your job, anything

. . . and especially any higher power you may have believed in, for allowing this terrible thing to happen to you.

- Suspecting that if only your doctor were more knowledgeable, he could tell you what to do to get better faster.
- Resenting the health and good fortune and smiling faces of others.
- Feeling as if whatever you are going through today is never going to end or change.
- Wanting to cry, or scream, or something—but not being able to.
- Feeling old beyond your years.
- Being embarrassed by your weakness.
- Having a short memory span and a short attention span.
- Sensing that you're not "doing it right," that somebody else would know how to be sick better than you do.
- Being anxious that you are wasting time.
- Wishing you could pray or be more patient or virtuous, and yet not being able to change.
- Imagining the worst. Fantasizing about all the things your doctor is not telling you.
- Entertaining thoughts of suicide.
- Sensing that something bigger and stronger and more ultimate than you has the upper hand in your life.
- Finding that your mind is repeating negative, energy-draining messages over and over again.
- Feeling stiff and sore all over and wishing you could exercise more.
- Fearing the unknown.
- Developing an awesome respect for the body and a fear of how powerful it can be.
- Being afraid to eat or drink or move for fear of doing damage to yourself.
- Feeling overwhelmed by the amount of conflicting data about nutrition, exercise, and other aspects of healing that you come across.
- Expecting other people to read your mind and know what you need, so you don't have to ask.
- Disappointment at who isn't concerned about you, who doesn't reach out to you at a time like this.
- Wanting to isolate yourself, to just crawl into a hole and heal the way an animal does, without having to ask anything of anybody.

- Feeling bad because your visitors are tedious and you hate to ask them to leave.
- Difficulty sleeping at night.
- Trying to do too much too soon.
- Feeling like you're babying yourself, and not liking it.
- Sensing that nobody else really understands what it is that you are going through—not your mate, not your doctor, not your nurses . . . nobody.
- Thinking that if only this had happened at another time you would have been able to handle it better.
- Resenting the suddenness of this change of life circumstances. Feeling the injustice of it.
- Losing your sense of humor. Taking everything very seriously.
- Waking up in panic, thinking about things that never bothered you before.
- Living in fear that the same thing (accident, heart attack, illness) could happen at any moment again.
- Recognizing that this could be one of the most valuable life experiences you've ever had—but being unsure of what to do about that.

And there you have it.

R_x 2: SORTING OUT CONFUSION AND CONFUSING FEELINGS

We often don't know what it is we *are* feeling, or we have so many feelings that we get lost in confusion and even panic. It is therefore important to sort out what is going on inside your heart and mind. Knowing your feelings makes it easier to express yourself, to find out what you want, and to ask for what you need. This exercise will help you in that process.

1. Read over the statements below and check the ones you relate to most strongly now.

    _____ I feel lonely.　　　_____ I feel scared.
    _____ I feel confused.　　_____ I feel unloved.
    _____ I feel unlovable.　 _____ I am a burden to
    _____ I feel embarrassed.　　　others.

_____ I feel weak

_____ I feel angry at others.

_____ I feel bored.

_____ I feel guilty.

_____ I feel regretful.

_____ I feel numb.

_____ I feel insignificant.

_____ I feel ugly.

_____ I feel anxious.

_____ I feel stupid.

_____ I feel depressed.

_____ I feel insecure.

_____ I feel angry at myself.

_____ I feel frustrated.

_____ I feel sorry for myself.

_____ I feel resentful.

_____ I feel sad.

_____ I feel useless.

_____ I feel powerless.

_____ I feel irritable.

_____ I feel somber and serious.

_____ I feel restless.

_____ I feel panicked.

2. Begin to explore the basis for each of the feelings you identify with by adding the word *when* to the feeling phrase, and then completing the sentence in as many ways as you can.

    For example:

I feel scared when my regular doctor isn't here.

I feel scared when I don't really know what is wrong with me.

I feel scared when my children are home alone.

I feel scared when . . .

3. Bringing to light some of the situations or thoughts that occasion your feelings is a helpful strategy. It allows you to move from that vague, overwhelming sense of confusion and panic to knowing that you may begin to *do something about them.* For example, you can try the following:

Share them with a trusted friend.

Ask for specific help.

Handle whatever you can do for yourself.

Allow the feelings to be there, while you just watch them as if they were part of a movie.

Entrust yourself to a higher power.

This exercise requires some discipline on your part. It is much easier to stay confused than it is to move forward and face life. The result of clarifying your feelings in this way is well worth the effort.

R_x 3: OPTIONS FOR EXPRESSING ANGER

Anger may come up a lot when you're sick. Why? Because illness changes your life in undesirable and unanticipated ways, and you don't like it. This causes you to feel angry.

It is helpful to know that anger is often a cover-up for other emotions, especially unfamiliar feelings that may be very difficult to face, such as hurt, guilt, helplessness, fear, or remorse. Chances are very good that if you are angry, it is your way of dealing with one of these other feelings. So what do you do?

First, recognize that there is probably something you want or need, like consolation and encouragement, or more information, or a way to start reclaiming some control of your life. Anger is a great gift—a clue to deeper needs and a cue to discovering what is actually running you.

Firing your anger in the direction of the person or event that occasioned it may serve only to frustrate you further and create more anger. Expressing the *root* of the anger brings the real wound to light and allows you to address it directly.

I am strongly in favor of releasing angry energy in some nondestructive way, such as vigorous breathing, exercising, or hitting the bed. Here are a few ways to release the energy:

Shake it off. Check with your doctor first if you have any doubts about your ability to participate in vigorous breathing or movement. If you can use your hands or feet, try shaking them as if you were trying to shake off something that had stuck to you. Or beat on your bed with your hands or feet. Slap it, pound it, or hit a pillow. Bite your sheets . . . hard. Ask for some modeling clay and knead it mercilessly. In short, do anything that allows you to give vent to feelings that you don't know what to do with, as long as it isn't destructive. Give yourself permission to be wild. You may be surprised to find that laughter erupts more often than you would have expected. Rage and laughter are close friends. Accept them both.

Cool yourself down. Water is the key to this one. Go wash your hands or take a shower or bath if possible. Let your anger be loosened and washed away with the soap and water. Also, try drinking several glasses of water. Additional water in your system will help you to clean from the inside out.

Write a letter. Express your anger in your journal. Spare nothing as you write. If you can't write, speak your letter out loud to yourself. When it is complete, destroy the letter in some way. Sometimes marking all over it with thick, heavy strokes of a crayon or scribbling all over it with a pen or pencil will create a valuable sense of relief.

Make an angry picture. On paper, draw figures or symbols, or just write particular words that represent your anger. Make the picture angry!

Act out or express your anger with a friend (but not the one you're angry at). Perhaps the gentlest way to express "hot" feelings is to act them out in some of the ways suggested above, but to do it in the presence of a friend who is accepting and unafraid. In fact, inviting someone to scream or "vent" with you can be a form of play. Why not just scream or breathe or drink water until you're both laughing?

Last, finish off any releasing session by nurturing yourself in every way. Snuggle up with your teddy bear and take a nap. Call a friend and talk or ask for a massage. Above all, congratulate yourself for your willingness to be a feeling human being.

Developing Relaxation

BREATHING TO RELAX

The breath is life. The more completely you breathe, the more oxygen your cells receive and therefore the more life-force you feel throughout your whole body. And there are additional advantages to breathing well, like stress reduction. The following exercises use breathing to help you achieve a more relaxed state of mind.

Watching the breath. By observing how you breathe, you relax yourself and also heighten overall awareness. This is why breath watching is a meditation practice too. Here's how to watch the breath:

1. Begin by breathing normally for a few minutes and simply observe what is going on. Do not try to change anything. Just watch. Note the following as your breathe:

   Do you breathe with both your nose and your mouth, or only one?
   When you inhale, how far down does the air go? To your throat? To your chest? To your abdomen?
   What, if anything, moves as you breathe? Shoulders? Chest? Diaphragm?

2. As you become aware of the gross movements involved in breathing, you can now refine your focus. Remember, don't try to change anything. Just observe.

   Is there any subtle difference between the temperature of the inhaled air and the exhaled air?
   Are your inhalations longer than your exhalations, or vice versa?
   Is there more openness in one nostril than in the other? Which is clearer?

Has your breathing changed at all since your started watching it? In all likelihood, it has slowed down and deepened.

Use breath watching whenever you wish to calm yourself.

The balanced breath. Focusing attention on the length of the inhalation, the length of the exhalation, and the length of the pause between the two is another breathing exercise that will help you relax. (Note that this is not recommended as the way to breathe all the time, but only as a specific exercise.) Here's what to do:

1. Begin by letting go of the air currently in your lungs. Expand your belly to help push it out.
2. Start to inhale, slowly, counting to eight as you do (one . . . and . . . two . . . and . . .).
3. After you reach eight, hold your breath to the same count of eight.
4. When complete with that cycle, gradually exhale to that same slow count of eight. Exhaling slowly is often the most difficult part for many people. Perhaps you are used to blowing your air out in one great puff, so this modified exhalation process is a bit of a challenge. Don't strain. If you can only get to four before you feel the need to inhale again, that's okay.
5. Breathe naturally for a minute or so, then repeat the whole cycle.
6. Repeat the cycle two to four times more, using natural breathing for a minute or so between each balanced breath cycle.

Breathe the light of health. Read this over before you actually do it. Or have a friend read it to you. This exercise will help you to relax by "directing" your inhaled air to any part of the body that is particularly tense, like the shoulders.

1. Sit or lie down in a comfortable position. Close your eyes.
2. Breathe in. Imagine that you are sending the inhaled air directly to your shoulders (or whatever other part is in need of relaxing).
3. Imagine seeing a faint light or tiny candle flame in the center of the tense body-part.
4. As you inhale, "feed" that light or flame with your inhaled

breath, and watch as it begins to grow brighter and then to expand in size. You may notice that a pleasant warmth starts to develop in the area of your focus.

5. Make the connection in your mind between the growth of this light and the relaxation of your tension. As the light increases in size and intensity, you tension is diminished.

6. Keep breathing until the light fills your whole body inside, and then watch as it penetrates your skin from the inside out and begins to form a glow or aura all around the outside of your body.

7. Rest and breathe normally in the aura created by this light.

8. After a few minutes, complete this exercise by beginning to stretch your fingers and toes, your hands and feet. Stretch your neck, your face, and whatever else wants to move. Slowly open your eyes.

Breathing worry away. Before your confinement, your normal physical exercise and work gave you some chance to naturally let off steam. Now, since you are less mobile, you need to use conscious breathing as a steam valve to release your stored-up tension and emotional pain. Try this technique: Take a series of short, quick breaths. Inhale only through your nose. Exhale through the mouth as if you were trying to blow out a candle at the foot of your bed. Do this six or seven times in succession. Imagine that the candle is a worry or problem. As you blow it out, feel it being released from your body and mind as well.

PROGRESSIVE RELAXATION

Progressive relaxation is a method that teaches you to discriminate between the feelings of tension in your muscles and the feelings of relaxation when that tension is temporarily released. This is valuable because many of us don't even know how tense we are most of the time, and therefore have difficulty knowing how to relax.

To do progressive relaxation, systematically tighten, hold, and then release the muscles in various parts of the body. If you experiment with this method, remember that it is not a weight-lifting contest, but rather an exercise in developing awareness. Don't strain yourself, especially if parts of your body are still healing from surgery. Tiny movements, tiny contractions will do as much as big ones in teaching you these differences.

1. Inhale and then continue to hold your breath while you tighten your right arm. Make a fist and let the tension develop in your wrist, your forearm, your elbow area, and your bicep. When your entire arm is tense, release your breath and the muscular contraction all at once. Attend, by awareness, to how this arm now feels, especially in contrast to the other arm. Repeat the process.
2. Then go on and do the same with your left arm. Repeat. Note the difference in the way your arms feel as compared with the way your legs feel.
3. Work then with each leg, then in turn with the abdomen, the chest, the shoulders and back, the neck, the face.
4. Conclude by resting and sensing your body from head to toe.

Practice of this type, besides being relaxing, helps you to know yourself and to develop a greater sense of self-control.

PALMING TO RELAX

This simple technique for relaxation makes use of breathing, visualizing, and cutting off of sensory stimulation to the eyes.

1. Rub the palms of your hands together to warm them.
2. Place one cupped palm over each eye, the fingers of one hand crossing the fingers of the other hand on your forehead.
3. Keep your eyes open. Arrange your palms so that no light can be seen.
4. Breathe softly and deeply for eight breaths, feeling warmth rising in your arms, your hands. Experience this warmth bathing your eyes.
5. At the same time, imagine a happy and peaceful scene from your past when you felt good.
6. After the eight breaths, remove your hands from your eyes and look softly around the room.

Pain Control Techniques

A SIMPLE ACUPRESSURE TREATMENT

This system of applying finger pressure to points on the body can alleviate pain and open energy channels. It is based on a model that views the body as a network of energy pathways, called meridians. Illness, tension, and fatigue are all related to a blocking of the energy flow along these meridians. By applying finger pressure to specific points, these blockages are relieved, pain is reduced, and the natural flow of energy is restored.

Here are a few basic guidelines in giving yourself a simple acupressure treatment:

- *Trust yourself.* You do not need extensive training to know where pressure points and meridians are located in your body. Explore the areas suggested here to find the sensitive spots. They are the pressure points in the meridians.
- *Don't press too hard.* Too much direct pressure can cause added tension. Start with a gentle touch at first and then increase pressure slightly, going deeper into the body as the muscle relaxes.
- *Tune in to your body.* The changes you feel may be quite subtle, but their effects can be powerful. Do not expect anything, but be aware of what does happen.

Head and Neck Relaxation

1. Using the middle finger of each hand, apply light pressure to the most sensitive area of your temples. Hold there until you feel relaxation.
2. With the middle finger of each hand, find the sensitive areas along the base of the skull and down the back sides of the

neck. Hold these points or gently massage in a circular motion with all four fingers.

3. Tension is often held in the jaw. With the middle finger, find the sensitive area on the jaw joint and hold. You may want to apply increasing pressure as the jaw relaxes.

For Headache and Sinus Congestion

1. With your thumbs, apply pressure to the inside eye socket, at the bridge of the nose.
2. With the middle finger, apply pressure to the sides of the nose just under the bridge. Again, feel around for the most sensitive spot. This may stop a sneezing fit or clear up congested nasal passages.

The techniques of acupressure, shiatsu, do-in, myotherapy, and others are all valuable for pain control. They each require attention and practice. Check your local library or bookstore for literature that can teach you about these approaches.

ADDITIONAL SUGGESTIONS FOR PAIN CONTROL

- Heat is often helpful for chronic pain, since it helps muscles to relax. Use a hot shower or bath as your therapy, or soak towels in warm water to which some fresh-grated ginger root has been added. Wring out and apply hot towel to the area of pain. (Note of caution: People with certain allergies, clotting defects in the blood system, certain types of malignancies, and severe depression should consult with a physician before using heat treatment for pain.)
- Try using cold compresses or even ice massage on the area of pain. Acute pain seems to respond generally well to this natural form of anesthetic. (Caution here: Don't overdo your use of ice on the skin, as frostbite could result. Also, those with rheumatoid arthritis or allergies that produce hives are advised against prolonged cold. Some people do develop blood clotting abnormalities from exposure to extreme cold.)
- Massage the painful place, or else move your hands in a circu-

lar motion in the air *above* the painful area. This massages the "aura" and can be as soothing as direct physical contact.

■ Experiment with applying pressure to sensitive areas on your feet or hands, since these may be connection points for pain in other parts of the body. See the section on foot massage and hand massage in appendix E.

■ Carry on a conversation with your pain, or else write out a dialogue with it in your journal. Ask it why it is here now, what it has to teach you, and how it can be alleviated.

■ Refer back to appendix C and use relaxation and breathing exercises to help alleviate your pain. In appendix J, the Imaging Flip exercise is specifically applicable to pain control.

■ Place your focus on pleasure. Devise any means available to pleasure yourself.

*Exercise and Play
for the Body in Bed*

As you approach this section, keep several things in mind:

- ■ *Check with your doctor.* If you're unsure of what you should or shouldn't do, it's important to ask.
- ■ *Take it easy.* Move slowly, without jerking, pushing, or forcing anything, and you should have no trouble with the exercises suggested here. Be graceful, gentle, "light" with yourself, and you'll have a great time as well.
- ■ *Start small.* Even if you can move only one finger or one eyeball, do it. It is important to keep moving, and also to remember that tiny movements can have great effect on the overall flexibility and balancing of the whole body.
- ■ *Listen to your body.* Be a friend to yourself and observe warning signals. Learn to distinguish between helpful pain and harmful pain. It always taxes you somewhat to stretch, especially if you haven't been doing it lately. In general, try going to the point where you *feel* the stretch or the pull, but don't push that stretch so that it becomes pain. Hold the stretch for a few moments while you keep breathing into it. In time, you will notice that you are stretching even farther.
- ■ *Remember to breathe.* The more oxygen your muscles get, the better they will respond. Many of the exercises here contain suggestions for coordinating the breath with the movement.

This appendix is divided into three parts: The first contains a basic workout program consisting of a series of exercises for stretching and strengthening all parts of your body.

The second is for fun. Included are directions for giving yourself or another a foot or hand massage. These techniques provide you with an opportunity to "touch" your whole body by stimulating corresponding points on the hand or foot. You will definitely want to experiment with this.

The third and last part contains some methods of instant soothing and ways to nurture yourself. These postures are extremely beneficial when you are feeling depressed or discouraged.

1: STRETCHING AND STRENGTHENING IN BED

Here is a basic exercise program to be done in bed. The general routine stretches and strengthens every part of the body. Because it is not possible to present specific exercises here for all kinds of health conditions, it is important that you remember the following:

- Use these exercises as suggestions. Use whatever you can, and disregard the rest.
- Be creative. Devise stretches of your own.
- Check with your doctor if you have any question about what is good for you.

Ankle Flex and Ankle Rolls

1. Lie flat on your back. Inhale and flex your feet, pointing toes up toward your knees. Let heels lift an inch or so from the bed.
2. Now exhale and flex feet in the other direction, pointing toes toward the foot of the bed. Repeat 1 and 2 ten times. Rest.
3. Inhale as you rotate both ankles in circles to the right, three to five times. Imagine that you are drawing circles with your big toes.
4. Exhale as you reverse the motion, rotating both ankles in circles to the left, three to five times. Repeat twice.
5. Rest; breathe normally.

Inner Leg Isometrics

1. Lie flat on your back and stretch your legs out, with your feet a few inches apart. Inhale, then squeeze your feet, knees, and thighs together.
2. Exhale and release. Repeat five times.

Thigh Stretch and Strengthener

1. Lie on your back with your right knee bent to support your lower back and your right foot on the bed. Extend the left leg.
2. Inhale and raise the left leg about six inches off the bed. Hold for a count of five.
3. Exhale. Lower your leg to the bed. (Take it easy on this one. Work up to it by raising your leg only an inch or two to start.)
4. Take a three-foot strap, belt, or rope. Loop it around the foot of your extended leg and pull your foot slowly toward your head. Keep your back and head on the bed. Hold in this position while you take five slow and gentle breaths. Release slowly.
5. Repeat on the other leg.

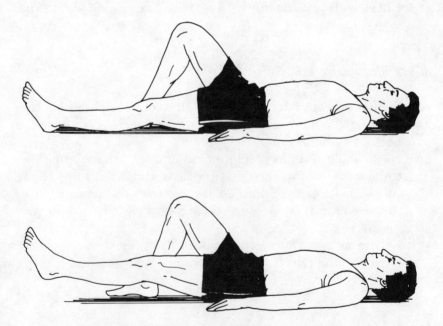

Thigh Stretch and Strengthener

Thigh Stretch and Strengthener (continued)

Pelvic Lift (for Lower Back, Buttocks, and Legs)

1. Lie on your back and bend your knees, keeping your feet close to your buttocks. Keep arms and hands palm down, next to your hips.
2. Inhale and lift your pelvis slowly toward the ceiling, keeping shoulders, neck, and throat relaxed and resting on the bed.
3. Hold this position for three to four slow breaths.
4. Exhale slowly and lower yourself one vertebrae at a time, until your buttocks rest on the bed. Repeat three times.

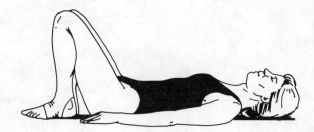

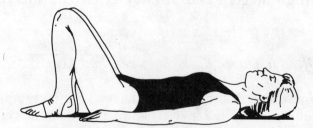

Pelvic Lift

Knee Hug (*for Lower Back*)

1. Lie on your back, knees bent. Inhale, drawing knees up toward your chest. Clasp your arms around your knees and squeeze.
2. As you exhale, draw knees even closer in toward your chest.
3. Rock slowly and gently from side to side. Breathe evenly for ten to twenty seconds.
4. Inhale, releasing your legs slowly. Exhale, lowering your feet to the bed and straightening your legs.

Knee Hug

Lower Back Twist

1. Lie on your back and place your feet flat on the bed, knees bent. Arms along your sides, about one foot from the body.
2. Inhale and place the right leg over the left, at knee level.
3. Exhaling slowly, allow the legs to fall to the left side. Keep both shoulders on the bed as much as possible, but without pulling or straining, as your legs drop. This will allow for a stretching in the lower spine. Hold for several seconds, breathing evenly, relaxing into position.
4. Inhale. Come back to center very slowly. Uncross your leg and repeat the full sequence on the other side.

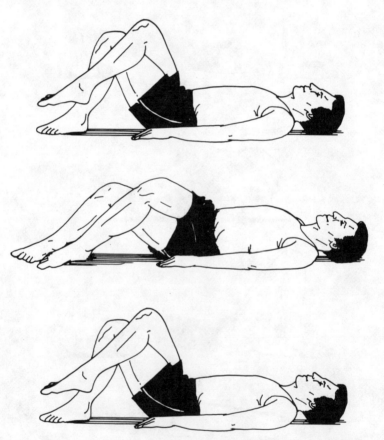

Lower Back Twist

Abdominal Strengtheners

1. Lie on your back. Take a few deep, full breaths.
2. Clasp hands behind your head, elbows out to the side. If you can raise your legs, put them up in the air, with knees bent, at about a 60-degree angle from the bed. Cross your ankles. (If you can't raise your legs, then bend your knees, placing your feet flat on your bed. Now cross legs at the ankles.)
3. Inhale, raising head, neck, and chest toward knees. Hold for a count of five.
4. Exhale and slowly lower your upper body to the bed. Repeat three to five times, slowly.

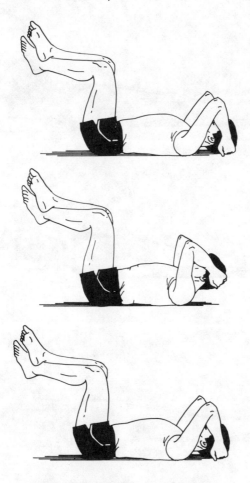

Abdominal Strengtheners

Fish Pose (for Upper Back)

1. Lie flat on your back with arms close to your sides.
2. Inhale and rise up onto your elbows. Rest your forearms on the bed.
3. Exhale and slowly lower your head back so that the crown of your head points back toward the bed. Hold. Breathe three to four times, normally.
4. Inhale, bringing your chin back toward your chest.
5. Exhale. Gently lower your upper back until it rests on the bed again. That should feel good!

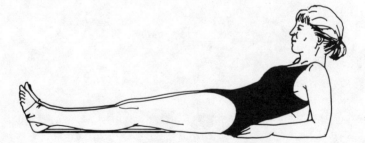

Fish Pose

Face, Head, and Neck Stretches

1. Lie on your back, open eyes wide, and stick out your tongue, pointing it toward your chin. Stretch every muscle in your face as tightly as you can. Hold for ten seconds. Release.
2. Clasp your hands behind your head. Inhale, lifting your head to put your chin on your chest. Hold for three slow, full breaths. Exhale, lowering head to the bed. Repeat three times.
3. Inhale; roll your head slowly to the left. Exhale, roll head slowly to the right. Repeat five times.
4. Imagine that you have a pencil protruding from your chin. Inhale, turn your head to the left, and begin to draw the largest circle you can using that pencil. Halfway around your circle, exhale slowly as you continue drawing. Make three circles to the left, and then rest for ten to fifteen seconds. Then make three circles to the right. Keep your breathing coordinated as much as possible. Feel how good it is to stretch your neck and head in this way.

Total Body Stretch

1. Lie on your back. Stretch and rest your arms above your head.
2. Push your feet and hands in opposite directions, as if you were being stretched. Breathe normally and hold this stretch for about ten seconds.
3. Relax. Repeat three times.

2: SELF-MASSAGE

Foot Treatment

In *The Foot Book,* author Devaki Berkson writes:

> Otau was a wise, old, and wrinkled man. The whole village respected his healing abilities. One day a foreigner came to ask him many questions and write down the healing ways of Otau. However, all Otau would say was, "See to their feet and you have seen to their body." "I do not understand," insisted the foreigner. "Your under-

standing will never be enough," Otau chuckled. "See to their feet, and that will be enough."

Foot reflexology, or zone therapy, is the correct terminology for this type of pressure-point treatment. The theory behind reflexology is that the body is divided lengthwise into energy zones that end at the feet. Here, then, are located reflex points that correspond to all major organs, glands, and body parts. Attention to the zones on the feet can thereby affect the whole body. Perhaps this is what Otau was referring to. Reflexologists attest to the overall therapeutic value of this type of treatment. It relaxes, stimulates energy flow, and often relieves pain and congestion in the body.

1. Position yourself so that you can comfortably hold one of your feet in both hands. This can be done more easily if you can sit in a chair. Some of you will need to invite a friend to give you this foot treatment.
2. Now, begin to massage this foot and ankle gently all over. Work between and around your toes. Give special attention to your ankles.
3. Using your thumb pads or the knuckle of your index finger, begin to explore your foot and ankle until you encounter a sore spot. Apply light pressure here and massage in a circular motion for no more than thirty seconds at a time. Then move on to find another spot that needs attention.
4. The chart on the opposite page will indicate the places on your foot that correspond to the rest of your body.
5. When you are finished, stretch your toes. Bend, flex, and rotate your ankle. Gently rub your foot all over . . . and then go to work on the other foot.

A Healing Hand Massage

Even if you can't reach your feet, you can experience the benefits of full-body massage by working on your hands. Like the feet, the hands contain points that correspond to every part of the body.

- Use a lotion or light oil to soothe and soften hands as you massage them.
- Work on all parts of your hands: palms, top sides, and all over

FOOT REFLEXOLOGY

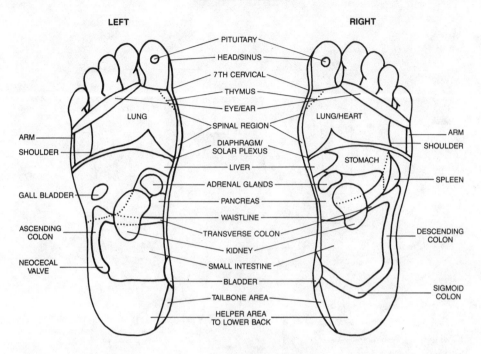

LEFT　　　　　　　　　　　　　RIGHT

PITUITARY
HEAD/SINUS
7TH CERVICAL
THYMUS
EYE/EAR
LUNG　　SPINAL REGION　　LUNG/HEART
ARM
SHOULDER
DIAPHRAGM/
SOLAR PLEXUS
STOMACH
LIVER
ADRENAL GLANDS
PANCREAS
WAISTLINE
TRANSVERSE COLON
KIDNEY
SMALL INTESTINE
BLADDER
TAILBONE AREA
HELPER AREA
TO LOWER BACK

ARM
SHOULDER

SPLEEN

DESCENDING
COLON

SIGMOID
COLON

ARM
SHOULDER

GALL BLADDER

ASCENDING
COLON

NEOCECAL
VALVE

the fingers, including the fingernails and fingertips. Attend to the wrists as well.

- Use firm pressure, varied with lighter "smoothing" and "milking" motions.
- Whenever you encounter a spot of tenderness, stay there. Apply moderate pressure and then work the spot over with small, circular strokes.
- Stretch fingers by pulling firmly on them. Stretch wrists by bending them forward and backward, holding the extreme position for a few seconds and then releasing.
- Don't neglect to massage the flesh between your fingers.
- Occasionally, shake your hands briskly as if you were shaking off drops of water. This will energize your hands.
- To conclude, place one hand in the palm of the other, close your eyes, and rest.

The chart that follows indicates reflex areas—places that correspond to other parts of your body. Be sure to give special, *gentle,* attention to areas of your body most in need of healing now.

PALM REFLEXOLOGY

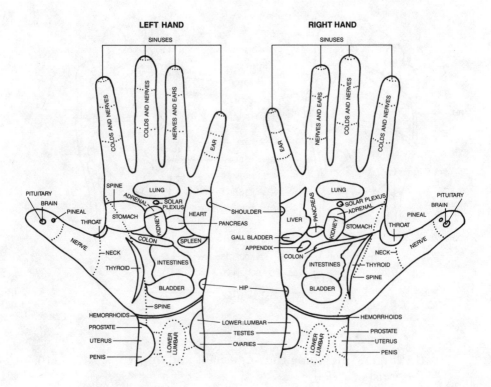

3: INSTANT SOOTHING

Sometimes all you want is a loving hand to hold. If that's not available, try the next-best thing: a few simple ways to soothe and nurture yourself.

Rock and Roll

1. Lie on your back, legs extended, breathing normally.
2. Place your left hand on the back of your neck, just under your skull. Place your right hand on your belly.
3. Now, rock your legs gently back and forth, breathing with slow, full breaths. Continue for one or two minutes.

Belly Release

1. Fill a hot-water bottle with medium-hot water.
2. Lie on your back, knees bent, feet flat on the bed.
3. Place the bottle (wrapped in a towel if desired) on your abdomen. Breathe normally as the warmth slowly relaxes your belly.

Head Ease

1. Lie on your back with your legs extended.
2. Place a folded, medium-hot washcloth over your closed eyes.
3. Massage your whole head and scalp. Breathe in the warmth. Let yourself sink deeply into the goodness of your own touch. Go on to massage your face and neck.
4. Rest.

Brightening Your Environment

> Whether people are fully conscious of
> this or not, they actually derive coun-
> tenance and sustenance from the "at-
> mosphere" of the things they live
> with.
>
> FRANK LLOYD WRIGHT

Your immediate environment is going to affect your mind, your body, and your spirit as you recuperate. Some surroundings raise your spirits, while others seem to drain your energy, agitate you, or depress you. Recognize, however, that everybody is different. For one person a busy room means creativity and excitement. For another it means anxiety. It all depends upon your individual taste and your tolerance.

Creating the atmosphere most conducive to healing is the task at hand. Use the questions that follow to begin making lists of any and all ways in which you can modify your surroundings to encourage restfulness, security, stimulation, and health.

- Is there enough open space in this setting? If not, what can be removed to allow for it?
- Is there too much space? If so, what would I like to fill it with? (Space is not simply empty-floor area. Look at the walls and ceiling as well. Are they too busy, too bare, or too boring? What needs to change, if anything?)
- Does this room reflect the richness and beauty of my person-ality?
- What colors are "healing colors" for me? Do I have enough of them?

- Would green plants or flowers be able to thrive in this environment? (If they couldn't, how can you expect to?)
- Are there healthy, interesting, and inspiring things to look at in this environment?
- What is the "audio" environment like? Noise levels? Opportunities for music? What kinds? What music feels healing to me?
- What does this place smell like? Is this healing for me? What is?
- If I could design the most perfect environment in which to make my recovery, what would it be like? What colors would I choose, what furniture? What sort of lighting, what kind of access or vulnerability to sound? Would I have living things? What's the view from the window? How accessible are the things I need?

Read back over your responses to the previous questions. Don't underestimate any idea or wish just because it seems impossible. Instead, use your visions as a trigger to challenge you to come up with practical changes that could produce the same or similar effects. Sometimes the tiniest modification, like a different bedspread or a colored light bulb, can make a tremendous change in the entire atmosphere of your room.

Keep this in mind as you read over the following possibilities:

- *Plants, plants, plants, flowers, and more plants.* Collect lots of them. Love them. Talk to them. You can grow an herb garden in an empty egg carton or old ice-cube tray on your window ledge. Herbs grow fast and smell great.
- *Living things.* Perhaps it's time to get that pet you've always wanted. A kitten? A few fish? A bird?
- *Posters and pictures.* Posters can be educational as well as decorative. You can lie flat on your back and study a map of the world, great wines of California, botany, or anatomy from a poster placed on the ceiling or the wall nearest you. How about a picture for that bare wall? Many public libraries will allow you to check out a painting. Change your pictures or murals regularly, or move them around to gain a whole new appreciation of them.
- *Let there be light.* Vary the light in the room by changing the

intensity or color of light bulbs, or by moving lamps around. If you have only fluorescent lighting in your room, ask for a lamp that has incandescent bulbs. Use it for a few days and experience the different effect it has on you.

- *Color.* Experiment and play as much as possible with this one. There is a whole science to color that you may know more about than you are aware of. When I was recuperating, for instance, I had a comforter that was tangerine colored on one side, magenta on the other; I could change my mood by simply turning it over. Be creative. Use colored cloths—tablecloths, bedspreads, wall hangings—to decorate walls, to cover old radiators, to replace curtains, to brighten the stand next to your bed. Ask to have your room painted. Paint a mural on your wall. Paint yourself a picture and put it up where you can see it.

- *Fragrance.* Incense, if used sparingly, can totally change the environment for the better, especially if your room tends to smell "sickly." Ask a friend to get you some sandalwood or floral incense. Room fresheners are available at all grocery stores. Fresh flowers and plants or herbs will create a pleasant aroma as well. How about using some fragrance on yourself— perfume, soaps, essential oils?

- *Your bed.* Since you may be spending a good deal of time in it, why not make your bed as colorful and sensuous as possible? Give special attention to the colors and especially the textures of your bedding—sheets, blankets, pillows, spread. If you have never used cotton flannel sheets, treat yourself. Comfortable even in the warmest weather, they provide a nurturing, soothing feeling.

- *Toys.* A bulletin board or blackboard is handy to have around. When I was laid up, a friend helped me brainstorm this book by writing our ideas on a blackboard. We also used it to play games on, like crosswords and tic-tac-toe. How about inviting a stuffed animal to share your bed? Or have some exercise equipment installed or brought in, just for the fun of it.

- *Music.* If you do nothing else, make sure you have access to music. Ideally, you should have a cassette unit within easy reach for playing music tapes, as well as recording possibilities so that you can make your own tapes if you wish. Tapes and tape recorders can be borrowed from libraries or friends. Refer to the list of recommended music tapes in appendix H, and sources of healing tapes and books on tape found in the Resource Guide at the back of the book.

- *What else?* Don't be stingy. This is your vacation, albeit a forced one. Splurge a little. The money you spend in enlivening your environment may well decrease what you will have to spend in painkillers or other drugs. So pleasure yourself.

❧

Amusements and Involvements

THE RECUPERATOR'S HOBBY/INTEREST CHECKLIST

Hobbies can be great fun. They can also be lifesavers when you have to remain confined for a while. If you don't already have a hobby, you probably have at least dreamed at some point of having unlimited time to explore an interest. Make this your chance to follow through on your wish.

The list that follows can be your first step. It is provided as a memory jogger to help you remember topics that might have ever interested you or hobbies you may have thought of pursuing.

The fact that you may not be able to actually go fly-fishing (or whatever other hobbies or interests you identify) need not discourage you. You can study up on the subject or practice tying flies even as you rest in bed.

Choose a few topics that grab you. Then consider what you can do to begin your exploration. Think of resources close by that you can check. Call your library or local college for references on the topic. Ask family members and friends if they have or can obtain books on the subject.

antiques	calligraphy	economics
archeology	carpentry	embroidery
architecture	cartooning	fishing
art	ceramics	flower arranging
astronomy	chamber music	flying
auto maintenance	chess	food preservation
backgammon	coin collecting	foreign languages
basket weaving	collages	furniture design
batik	computers	gardening
biology	crochet	gemstones
bonsai	doll collecting	genealogy
bridge	drawing	geography

geology	model building	real estate
history	mythology	recipes
home repair	needlepoint	robotics
hypnotism	opera	sailing
indoor plants	origami	Shakespeare
investing	painting	stained glass
jazz	philosophy	stamp collecting
juggling	physics	travel/adventure
landscaping	playwriting	weaving
literature	pottery	wine making
magic	psychology	yoga
math	quilting	

EMERGENCY FIRST AID FOR BOREDOM

- Design a game called Recuperation: For Patients and Care Givers. Try playing it with your visitors. If it's good, copyright it. Sell it. Make money.
- Design something to make your life easier or more pleasant as you recuperate. Many great inventions were so inspired.
- Try to remember the name or an impression of twenty men or women you've ever had for friends at any time in your life.
- Think of fifty restaurants you've eaten in, and try to remember what you ate, what the interior looked like, and who you were with.
- Compose your own "Bests" or "Worsts" list, including answers to such questions as What was the worst movie you ever saw? What was the best vacation you ever took? Who is your worst-dressed family member? What's the worst meal you ever had on Thanksgiving? and so on.
- Remember ten jokes. Think hard.
- Remember the ten happiest days of your life. What were they?
- Look in the business section of the white pages of your phone directory under "Dial -a- . . ." to find numbers for inspiring or interesting messages. Call and listen.
- Read your junk mail. Write letters back.
- Sometimes being clear about what you *don't* want inspires you to know better what you *do* want. Make a list of all the ways you definitely *do not* wish to spend your time (staring out the window; talking about Mildred's niece; watching TV reruns).

DRAWING AND COLORING

For those who can, drawing is rewarding and therapeutic when you are confined to bed. If you want to draw, keep in mind the following:

- Release all need to be an artist. Instead, return to being a four-year-old who draws only for pleasure.
- Use any medium available, preferably the one you are most comfortable with. These include pen, pencil, crayon, chalk, pastel, charcoal, or felt-tip marker. And of course there is always paint, water color, or oil.
- Before attempting to draw, always close your eyes and get in tune with your body. Breathe deeply for several moments.
- Hold your pen or pencil loosely, softly in your hand. Feel it as an extension of your body. Imagine that your blood and nerves and energy run into it.
- Choose colors that correlate with your mood and the subject you are considering.
- Before you actually mark the paper, let your imagination play with the infinite possibilities of form and color that are available to you.

Here are some suggestions for *what* to draw:

- Divide your paper in half. Draw yourself as you *feel now* on one side. On the other side draw yourself as you will be when *fully well.* Do not feel confined to drawing your image as a recognizable body. Be free to portray yourself in an abstract form.
- Draw your illness or accident. Again, use abstractions and symbolism as you wish. Now draw the healing agents that are eliminating the illness or accident. Show interaction between the two.
- Depict aliveness, or love, or forgiveness, or gratitude.
- Draw the interplay of life and death, health and disease, joy and sorrow.
- Draw any feeling you are currently enduring: aloneness, fear, anxiety, sadness, doubt, guilt, pain.
- Draw the world as you see it now. Then draw it as you wish it to be.

- Draw an ally—a friend, an angel, an animal, or a symbol that represents support, companionship, and unconditional love.
- Draw laughter, hilarity, silliness, absurdity.
- Draw a fantasy place of comfort and safety.
- Draw a dream sequence.
- Draw your own face, and have a conversation with it.

For a wonderful resource to the art of drawing, consult Betty Edwards' *Drawing on the Right Side of the Brain* (revised edition) (Los Angeles: Jeremy P. Tarcher, 1989).

If drawing is not your cup of tea, but if the idea of putting color on paper appeals to you, many wonderful coloring books for adults will inspire you and even teach you things as you work with them. Some of my favorites include anything by Ruth Heller, especially in the series Designs for Coloring (New York: Grosset and Dunlap); P. Kennedy's *North American Indian Design Coloring Book* (New York: Dover Publications); and M. Matt's *Human Anatomy Coloring Book* (New York: Dover Publications, 1982).

Music for Recuperation

The music selections contained here were chosen for their overall life-supporting quality. Rather than causing you to separate or dissociate from your body, these musical pieces will each encourage an alignment within you, helping you to harmonize yourself with the natural healing rhythm of your own body, and the real, healing energies of the earth. Anything by Vivaldi, Mozart, Bach, and other composers from the baroque period is highly recommended. All this music is vitalizing. It contains struggle at times, but is always victorious.

Below are my favorites:

Bach, *Double Concerto* or *Violin Concertos 1 and 2.* Stimulate joy, serenity, and a sense of radiance.

Bach, *Brandenburg Concertos.* Many excellent recordings. Tremendous variety. Experience a full range of feelings.

Mozart, *Violin Concertos 3 and 5.* Inspires magic, joy, and a sense of delight.

Pachelbel's Canon/Baroque Favorites. Soothing, full, rich, and life-supporting.

Chopin Nocturnes. Restful, dreamy, and peaceful.

Mahler, *Symphony no. 4.* Full of delightful, life-giving sounds.

Beethoven, *Symphony no. 6* (the *Pastoral*). Inspires happiness and contentment.

Dvořák, *Cello Concerto,* and Tchaikovsky, *Rococo Variations.* Full of richness, earthiness, and warmth.

Mendelssohn, *Violin Concertos,* and Tchaikovsky, *Violin Concertos.* Heart-filling, vibrant, and passionate.

❧

Support Networks and Services

BUILDING A SUPPORT LIST

Such a compilation can help you remember the people in your life who can be potential sources of assistance to you now or at some later time. Start to "build" your list by answering the questions presented here, and then transfer some of your responses to a master list, as suggested at the end of the exercise. You will be pleasantly surprised at how much you might otherwise have forgotten.

- Take a piece of paper and divide it into two columns. On the top of the left-hand column, write Places I Go. On the top of the right-hand column write People I Meet. Start by listing all the places you go to or went to regularly before your accident or illness. Include evening places as well as daytime places, places you go to regularly once a month, like a meeting of your church or social group, and even places you go to regularly but infrequently, as with that annual visit you make to Florida to visit your childhood friend.

  On the right side of the chart, list the people you regularly see or meet at the places you have indicated.
- Now take a fresh sheet to continue your list of contacts. Write the name of anyone you know who meets the following criteria. Consult the list you just made for additional names.

  trustworthy with money
  very good listener
  understanding and compassionate
  seems to enjoy helping others
  easy to be with
  makes me laugh
  very bright about practical matters
  offered help if I ever needed it

- Just in case you may have forgotten someone obvious, make a list of friends, colleagues at work, and relatives.
- Now that you have completed these memory-jogging lists, consider who may be available to you for ongoing or occasional support. Put a check or asterisk next to the names of those whom you would be comfortable either sharing with or asking for some help. Double the symbol for those you feel very comfortable about, and you will have your first-string support list.
- Now take a new sheet of paper and label it My Best Possible Supporters. Write the names of your first-string team, one name to a line. Follow with the list of your single-symbol supporters. You have now identified your best potential sources of support.

Using Your Support System

Remember that people like to help other people, especially when they are given a straight and direct way to serve.

Here are some ways to use your supporters' help:

Call these people when you need someone to talk to. Make sure to first ask if it is a convenient time for them to speak.

Call when you need help of some kind. (Refer back to the section Getting the Help You Need in "Step 4: Become an Active Partner," for reassurance in this.)

Invite these potential supporters to pay you a visit, to come to a party, to go out to lunch with you, to accompany you to a movie. Be creative.

OTHER SUPPORT SERVICES

General support services. These include counseling, financial aid, food, transportation, and so on. Save yourself a lot of time by speaking first to your doctor for help or referrals to agencies in your area that offer the kind of support or assistance you may need. Alternatively, call your minister, priest, or rabbi if you have a religious affiliation (or ever had a religious affiliation). "Social

Services" in the yellow pages will yield not only such religious community services, but more ecumenical groups and agencies as well that may be most helpful to you. If one group cannot help you, ask to be referred to someone who can.

And always approach friends and family.

Nursing. Consult the yellow pages under "Nurses" for home health care or occasional visiting nurses. But start by asking your doctor or friends for more personal recommendations.

Specific support groups. There are now thousands of support services and self-help organizations all over the country for people who have similar problems or experiences. They include such groups as Mended Hearts, for people who have had heart surgery or heart attacks; I Can Cope, for people who have cancer; and Reach to Recovery, for women who have had a mastectomy. Call your local newspaper to find out if they publish a directory of such groups.

Transportation. Many states offer handicapped-parking permits, which are for temporary disabilities too. To receive one, call your Department of Motor Vehicles for an application. You will fill out part of it and your doctor will fill out the rest. The permit, usually issued for ninety days, may be renewed.

Bus or ride services for the temporarily handicapped is also available. Call your local bus company (customer service department) and ask about the availability of ride services for the temporarily handicapped. Many offer reduced bus fares for the duration of the handicap.

The yellow pages of your phone book offers ride service information under "Handicapped Services."

Convenience products. Call or write for a free catalog of clothing for special needs, as well as self-help devices: Comfortably Yours, 61 W. Hunter Ave., Maywood, NJ 07607; 201-368-0400 (not a toll-free number).

Mental Imagery and Visualization

Mental visualization is the process of creating vivid pictures in your mind. Sense memory is a corollary process that allows you to "hear" and "taste" and "touch" those pictures as well.

Visualization and sense memory are used in many walks of life and have been shown to be extremely beneficial in improving all-around performance. Many athletes use visualization to rehearse their moves. Public speakers "see" themselves performing with poise and confidence. In the health profession, visualization is used to help people in childbirth, in weight control and smoke-ender programs, and even in cancer treatment.

For the recuperating person, developing your abilities to visualize and recall sensations will help you to

support your recuperation by bringing the mind into
   alignment with what the body is doing to heal itself;
make use of the many stress-reduction techniques that
   require the ability to "see with the mind's eye";
generate new ideas for application in all areas of your life;
   and have fun by expanding your creative imagination.

For example, if you know how your body is working to heal itself, such as in mending a bone, you can use visualization to encourage that process. If you know what a particular drug is doing, you can picture it attacking cells and destroying illness.

EXERCISE 1: FIRST STEPS IN VISUALIZING

Let's play with some simple visualization exercises. As you come upon the suggestion of a scene, close your eyes for about thirty seconds and closely examine the images your mind presents. Then proceed to "listen" to the sounds around. "Smell" the aromas; "feel" the textures; experience the temperature; "taste" things. Note any emotions or other memories that are aroused:

an ocean beach
a tropical rain forest
a mountain path leading to a clear lake by a waterfall
a flower display
a fruit stand

Try to use your visualization to experience the next images in detail and to carry them through to completion.

cutting a lemon and tasting the juice on your fingers
planting a seed and watching it flower
walking to the edge of the water and putting your feet in
taking a roller coaster ride at an amusement park
making love with your ideal lover

If you haven't stretched your sense, memory, and visualization muscles in a long time, you may have had difficulty with some of these images. Don't worry, though. You are doing more now than when you started this section. Keep practicing the above scenes until you feel comfortable with the process. At that point, you will be ready to continue to the next exercise in using visualization to improve your recuperation.

EXERCISE 2: MIND UNWIND

"Mind wind," commonly called worry or tension, has a great impact on the body and the soul. Repeatedly thinking of all the things you aren't getting done soon produces a tight knot in the pit of your stomach and a gnawing sense of frustration. When "mind wind" strikes, use some of the following "mind unwind" visualization approaches to relax and nourish yourself.

These exercises may be more enjoyable if you have someone read them to you. Ask a trusted friend or a nurse to play some soft music and then to quietly instruct you in relaxation, using my suggestions. Or you may want to make a tape recording of these for yourself so that they are available whenever you need or want them.

- *Go Sailing.* Water has universal appeal as a symbol of rest and relaxation, of rebirth and rejuvenation. One way to ease the wound-up mind is to take it to the beach or to the edge of a stream, waterfall, or clear mountain lake. To begin, find a comfortable position, either sitting up or lying down. Let your weight be supported by whatever you are sitting or lying on. Take a breath and allow yourself to feel the support of your chair or your bed. Sink into it. Take a few more deep and full breaths, and then allow your eyes to close. In your imagination, journey to a place near the water—that stream, waterfall, ocean, or lake. Look around you and notice colors, shapes, textures. Now notice the surface of the water. At first, imagine that the water is moving, active. Imagine that the surface of the water is your own mind. Continue to breathe slowly and deeply, all the while watching as the water begins to calm, first at the surface and then into its depths. Keep up the slow, deep breathing. Continue seeing the smooth, calm water until you experience your mind calm and peaceful as well. Now stay here for a while. As you prepare to leave this imaginary place, begin to slowly stretch your hands and feet, your fingers and toes. Gently open your eyes, slowly, a little at a time.
- *Healing Messenger.* Be comfortable. Breathe with intention, watching the rise and fall of your chest or abdomen. Let your tension go on the exhaled breath. Pause. Picture in your head a tiny messenger. This may be a tiny human figure or a symbolic representation like a spot of light. Send this messenger as a runner from your brain down into the tips of your toes. Have this runner announce to your toes that they can relax, that the crisis is over. Let the messenger stay in your toes until you can feel that they have gotten the message. Pause. Then have the messenger move up into your feet and ankles and do the same thing. Stay there until your feet and ankles have fully received the message to relax. Now send the messenger to your calves, your knees, your thighs . . . and so on throughout your whole body. Do both sides of the body at once, or else start up one side and down the other. Continue until your entire body is relaxed. Stay in this state for a while. When you are complete, begin to come back by stretching your fingers and toes, your hands and feet. Stretch any other part that feels like it. Begin to open your eyes a sliver at a time, as if the sun were coming up in the morning.

■ *Inner Dance.* Switch on the radio and tune in to a station that plays soft, relaxing music. Even better, play a tape or record of gentle music, like some of those suggested in appendix H. Close your eyes and breathe deeply. In your imagination, find yourself alone on a huge dance floor. You are dressed in flowing clothes. As the music plays, watch yourself move to it. Dance more beautifully than you have ever danced before. Don't confine yourself to the floor. Fly! Move out into space and dance among the stars. See yourself vibrant, healthy, graceful. Make big movements. Be free . . . wild . . . unrestrained. Move in brand-new ways. And keep on dancing. Breathe this picture of yourself into every cell of your body. Each cell is another universe in which you are the sole and gracious dancer.

EXERCISE 3: IMAGING FLIP

This visualization exercise is designed to help you "flip" the negative images you associate with your pain, tension, or discomfort into healing images. Making use of all your sensory modalities, it is extremely powerful. I have used it many times myself.

Begin by attending to the area of your body where the worst pain in located. Ask yourself the following questions:

■ If I were to draw a picture of my pain, associating it with some object or condition, what would that picture be? Tight-knotted nautical ropes, perhaps, or a murky, stagnant pool?
■ Is there a sound connected with the problem or pain? A grinding, perhaps, or a gurgling?
■ Is there a texture associated with it? A sore throat, for instance, might feel like tough sandpaper; an upset stomach might feel slimy.
■ Is there a temperature associated with it? A headache might feel hot; a broken limb might feel cold.
■ Is there a smell or taste associated with it?
■ Is there a movement associated with it? Churning, stabbing, pounding?

Now we will "flip" these images. The essential consideration here is what the problem or pain will look, feel, smell, sound, and taste like *when it is alleviated or cured.* For each image that you formed in answering the questions above, you will now substitute its opposite. For example, those knotted ropes are slowly untied and loosely laid out on the deck; the stagnant pool is drained and filled with clear, sweet water; the dark cloud of pain in your head is penetrated with sunlight; the pounding sound is replaced by the sound of a waterfall.

As you relax, substitute a positive, healing image for each negative, painful one. Use words if necessary to reinforce this. ("My head is filled with billowy, white clouds," for example.)

Post a sign or note close to you to remind yourself to flip often into your new set of images. Don't be discouraged if you can't conjure up all the images suggested. Use the ones that are strongest for you and be patient with yourself in anticipating results.

EXERCISE 4: VISUALIZE STRONG, HEALING WORDS

This exercise uses visualization to improve the power of words to convince your mind that you are healing.

1. Choose some strong words that evoke a sense of strength and healing in you. Words like *yes, alive, healthy.*
2. Imagine them on huge billboards all over the city in neon lights on the side of a building, or maybe carved out of the rock on the side of a mountain.
3. Take a favorite word for each day, allowing your choice of word to be determined by what you feel you need on that day.
4. Think of your word every chance you get throughout the day. See it often. Repeat the word or words to yourself as you go about your activities.
5. To reinforce this, write your word on several small cards or pieces of paper. Put them around where you will see them frequently. Each time you see them, remember your image of the word, say it to yourself, and feel it.

Meditation as a Way of Life

Meditation is a way of focusing within yourself, exploring your own inner landscape, or tilling the soil of your internal "garden" so that the seeds of conscious and compassionate living may grow.

To meditate is to be in relationship to life in all its simplicity, its color, its ordinariness, just as it is. Sometimes it's exhilarating, sometimes it's boring. What it feels like really doesn't matter so much. The meditator looks to see life clearly, in all its shades.

You never master meditation, just as you never master life. In this process of meditation, one is always a beginner. In fact, one of the great teachers of meditation, Suzuki Roshi, calls it "beginner's mind."

There are hundreds of approaches to meditation. Every major religion and countless spiritual groups recommend meditation in some form. Following are a few of the more practical approaches:

Prepare and drink a cup of tea. Then wash the pot and cup and put everything away. Perform each action with attention but not rigidity. If you notice that your mind is wandering from your activities, simply bring it back—again and again and again. If you do not like tea or cannot do all the work of making it, adapt this meditation with any kind of food or drink, even drinking a glass of water. The point is to stay conscious throughout.

Take a very, very slow walk. Walk with your eyes a bit lowered so that you will not be overstimulated by the things you see. As you walk, observe how you lift, move, and then place one foot after another on the ground. Observe how you breathe as you walk. Walk for ten minutes or so with attention. Do not be stiff. Do not worry if you lose your focus. Just come back to it again and keep walking. This is a very valuable exercise for those who are recuperating.

Listen. Sit or lie quietly and close your eyes. Imagine that you are a sonar scanning device. Extend the sensitivity of your hearing by alerting yourself to all the sounds in your environment. Keep making your ears "bigger" and more receptive. Note the farthest sound you can hear. Extend yourself to hear something beyond that. Focus in on one sound after another and just listen to it. Feel that sound resonate in your body. Slowly bring your awareness closer and closer to home. Listen so softly and delicately that you can hear the sounds of your own breathing. Keep your attention here. As your mind wanders, let it finish each thought it attaches to, and then bring it back to the focus on the sound of your breath.

Look. Use the figure below as a visual focusing device. Soften your eyes as you look at it. Look steadily but gently. Observe the many levels of organization that begin to emerge as you look. Draw no conclusions about anything. Just watch. Try gazing at a favorite object or picture or piece of art in the same way, without judgment.

Gaze. If you are close to a window or can go outdoors, use the sky, at night and during the day, as a source of meditation. Just look. Watch. Breathe. Observe where your thoughts take you. Don't try to restrict your thoughts. Give them the whole sky to play in.

These beginning meditations might seem a bit strange to you, but the simple awareness they aim toward is basic to every meditation form I have ever studied. What is important is *bringing meditation to life!*

Resource Guide:
Books and Tapes for Healing

Many books can help you as you heal. Some will help you pass the time, others will assist with specific problems. Still others will be like old friends, just keeping you company. If you can't get to a library or bookstore yourself, you may still be only a phone call away from getting the books you need.

Take advantage of the services offered by many libraries. Often they have a volunteer or homebound program that provides home delivery of the books you want. Call your local branch for information. Bookstores will often ship an order directly to your door. So call and inquire.

The following books were chosen for their "user-friendly" nature, which is very important for the recuperating person. Most contain both authoritative data and exercises for immediate application. I recommend them most highly; they have helped me.

GENERAL BOOKS

Colgrove, M.; Bloomfield, H., M.D.; and McWilliams, P. *How to Survive the Loss of a Love.* New York: Simon & Schuster, 1976. Yes, you have lost a "love" of some sort if you have endured a health crisis! The love lost may be a part of the physical body, a diminishment of functioning, or a loss of a dream or opportunity. Whatever it is, this simple book presents an easy and compassionate approach to integrating this loss into the rest of your life and then to moving on from it. The poetry of Peter McWilliams adds a dimension of heartfulness that you may be hungry for at this time. It is well named as a survival guide.

Cousins, N. *The Healing Heart: Antidotes to Panic and Helplessness.* New York: Avon Books, 1983. The famed editor of the *Saturday Re-*

view and author of *Anatomy of an Illness* (W. W. Norton, 1979) reveals his own process in recovery from heart attack in a way that is both inspirational and informative. Refusing to accept the status of "patient" or "invalid," Cousins engages his doctors and sets to work to dissipate the fear and panic that are so common at times like this. He lashes out at the impersonal and deadening approaches taken by the biomedical establishment in dealing with cardiovascular patients, while at the same time maintaining a balance of integrity with what is worthwhile in this system.

Moss, R., M.D. *How Shall I Live? Transforming Surgery or any Health Crisis into Greater Awareness.* Berkeley, Calif. Celestial Arts, 1985. All that the title suggests, and more. Moss is a doctor who now specializes in work that allows individuals to transform their thinking and energy patterns in relation to their illnesses or problems. This book encourages participation with your doctors and other care givers. The author recounts his own eye surgery as a potent example of establishing a partnership in healing. Later chapters provide exercises in writing, use of music in healing, and other nontraditional approaches to recovery. A book for recuperation and for the reorientation of life in general.

Rubin, T. I., M.D. *Reconciliations: Inner Peace in an Age of Anxiety.* New York: Berkley Books, 1980. This book saved my life at a time when I was seriously depressed and in need of straight-talking advice. Together with Stearns' book (see below), it is one that I use over and over and pass on to friends and students. Rubin takes an uncompromising look at our frantic, success-oriented culture and finds it seriously wanting. His book offers sound advice in how to counteract within yourself the anxiety-producing demands from outside. Touching on such topics as competition, time, money, relationships, and priorities, he directs the reader toward the state of "tranquil aliveness." As you recuperate, this book will cement a firm foundation for ongoing health and well-being.

Siegel, B., M.D. *Love, Medicine and Miracles.* New York: Harper & Row, 1986. This book is subtitled *Lessons Learned about Self-healing from a Surgeon's Experience with Exceptional Patients.* Siegel, a practicing physician and surgeon in New Haven, examines his exceptional cancer patients who have refused to retreat into passive acceptance of their diagnosis but rather engage in actively facing the odds and working to heal themselves. A book of encouragement for anyone, and particularly for a recuperating person who may be discouraged. Siegel places love and miracles on an equal footing with medicine. Using numerous case histories and personal examples, he explains how it is possible to do the impossible.

Stearns, A. K. *Living through Personal Crisis.* New York: Ballantine Books, 1984. The single most all-around helpful book in almost any situation, hands down. Required reading in the courses I have taught for years, it receives nearly unanimous appreciation from my students. I send it to friends who are troubled, to those who are being divorced or separated, and to those who are healing from illness. The book is about the losses that are a daily part of life, and what it takes to make it through crisis. The author writes with clarity, compassion, and enough authority to be reassuring. Readers will generally trust the very practical help she offers. Don't miss it.

Travis, J. W., M.D., and Ryan, R. S. *Wellness Workbook.* Berkeley, Calif.: Ten Speed Press, 1981, 1988. A book to guide you in the process of lifestyle change and to support you in self-appreciation, gentleness, and personal responsibility all along the way. Chapters deal with how to conserve and maximize energy in each life process, from breathing and eating through communication, sex, and the search for meaning and beyond. Practical exercises throughout. Easy to pick up and use. An excellent bedside companion and accompaniment to the work you are doing here.

TOPICAL SUGGESTIONS

Breathing

Smith, P. *Total Breathing.* New York: McGraw-Hill, 1980. Everything you ever wanted to know about breathing, and helpful ways to use it.

Depression

Berk, J. *The Down Comforter.* New York: Avon Books, 1980. Tiny steps can mean big changes. This book encourages you to start.

Exercise

Bell, L., and Seyfer, E. *Gentle Yoga.* Berkeley, Calif.: Celestial Arts, 1987. Written for the wheelchair-bound person, as well as those with arthritis, stroke damage, or M.S., the exercises in this book are recommended for recuperating people in general. Helps in strengthening and making flexibile all parts of the body. Yoga breathing and meditation also included.

Healing

Hay, L. *You Can Heal Your Life.* Santa Monica, Calif.: Hay House, 1987. The author cured herself after being diagnosed with terminal cancer. Her approach is one of turning around the disease-feeding mental programs that are a result of our belief systems. Uses positive self-talk, affirmations.

Simonton, O.; Matthews-Simonton, S.; and Creighton, J. *Getting Well Again.* Los Angeles: Jeremy P. Tarcher, 1978. Written primarily for the recovering cancer patient and family, this now-classic book is useful for anyone wanting to enhance medical treatment with relaxation and imagery techniques.

Heart Surgery

Cohn, K., M.D.; Duke, D.; and Madrid, J. *Coming Back: A Guide to Recovering from Heart Attack and Living Confidently with Coronary Disease.* Reading, Mass.: Addison-Wesley, 1987.

Hoffman, N. *Change of Heart: The Bypass Experience.* New York: Harper & Row, 1985. In-depth interviews with those who have been through it. People of all ages talk about the emotional as well as the physical repercussions.

Laughter

Peter, L. J., and Dana, B. *The Laughter Prescription.* New York: Ballantine Books, 1982. Everything you can imagine to get you to laugh, and more besides.

Massage and Touch

Krieger, D. *The Therapeutic Touch: How to Use Your Hands to Help or Heal.* Englewood Cliffs, N.J.: Prentice-Hall, 1979. Written for nurses and care givers, this book is a help to patients themselves as well.

Norman, L. *Feet First: A Guide to Foot Reflexology.* New York: Fireside Books, Simon & Schuster, 1988.

Meditation

Keating, T. *Open Mind, Open Heart.* Warwick, N.Y.: Amity House, 1986.

LeShan, L. *How to Meditate.* New York: Bantam Books, 1974.

Sujata, *Beginning to See.* San Francisco: Apple Pie Books, 1987.

Trungpa, C. *Shambhala: The Sacred Path of the Warrior.* New York: Bantam Books, 1986.

Pain Control

Bresler, D. *Free Yourself from Pain.* New York: Simon & Schuster, 1979. Still the best overall handbook around for dealing with pain. Provides instruction in the use of such alternative methods as journal keeping, visualization, exercise, and relaxation techniques.

Linchitz, R. *Life without Pain.* Reading, Mass.: Addison-Wesley, 1987. Deals extensively with the subject of endorphins.

Relaxation and Stress Reduction

Benson, H. *The Relaxation Response.* New York: Avon Books, 1975.

Davis, M. *The Relaxation and Stress Reduction Workbook.* San Francisco: New Harbinger Publishers, 1980. Something for everybody.

Visualization

Gawain, S. *Creative Visualization.* New York: Bantam Books, 1982. Combines use of both imagery and affirmation in teaching you how to use the mind for healing and more.

CASSETTES FOR HEALING, PAIN CONTROL, AND STRESS REDUCTION

Guided exercises that assist you in the healing process are available from Source Cassettes, P.O. Box W, Stanford, CA 94309. To order a tape or a catalog, call 800-52-TAPES. Composed and narrated by Emmett Miller, M.D., they are among the best I have encountered. I recommend the following:

Letting Go of Stress. Learn a logical progression from simple to sophisticated techniques for stress management. Four different methods for achieving deep relaxation. (#23)

Healing Journey. Learn techniques for active participation in your body's healing process. Valuable for acute or chronic conditions. (#16)

Successful Surgery and Recovery. Condition the mind and body to achieve maximum benefit and speedy recovery from surgery. Techniques to minimize anesthesia, postoperative swelling, pain, bleeding, and infection. (#203)

Change the Channel on Pain. Tune out pain and tune in relief. People with occasional or chronic pain can learn to "change the channel." (#46)

Environmental Sounds for Relaxation

Check your local record store for the Environments series or Solitude series recordings. You can order them yourself by calling Backroads Distributors at 800-825-4848. For a catalog, write Backroads, 417 Tamal Plaza, Corte Madera, CA 94925.

The natural sounds you can find in such pieces as *Slow Ocean, Wind in the Trees, Country Stream, Gentle Rain in a Pine Forest, English Meadow,* or *Thunderstorm in the Mountains* are excellent as background noise for recuperating people. They relax you and promote restful sleep. Your visitors will be calmed by them as well.

BOOKS ON TAPE

For those who are having difficulty in reading, holding a book, or keeping attention focused, books on tape are a godsend. Call your local public library to find out if they carry any, or inquire at a well-stocked bookstore in your area. If your local bookstore doesn't have the one you want, try the following:

Tattered Cover Bookstore, Denver, CO; 800-833-2327 (in Colorado, 800-821-2896).

Books on Tape, P.O. Box 7900, Newport Beach, CA 92658. Will ship anywhere in the United States. Tapes can be rented or purchased. To order tapes or a catalog, call 800-626-3333.

Audio Renaissance Tapes, 9110 Sunset Blvd., Ste. 200, Los Angeles, CA 90069; 213-273-9755. A fine selection of interesting and useful tapes, including "Getting Well" by Dr. O. Carl Simonton, as well as others by well-known authors in the field of health and well-being.